Yoga acts on my heart the way a loofah sponge does on my skin. My experiences become more immediate, engaging, and memorable as a result of sloughing off encrustations of habit and resistance. Gail Sher delineates, from among yoga's myriad possibilities, a series of exercises designed specifically for the artist. While writers are her stated audience, artists of all persuasions will benefit from yoga practice. The wisdom contained in this book will enrich their lives and thereby their work.

SUSAN WEBER, YOGA INSTRUCTOR,
BALLET TEACHER, AND FORMER MEMBER
OF THE LAR LUBOVITCH DANCE COMPANY

WRITING THE FIRE!

Yoga and the Art of
Making Your
Words Come Alive

GAIL SHER

BELL TOWER ✦ NEW YORK

Grateful acknowledgment is made for permission to reprint from:
Sam Hamill: "Zazen on Ching-t'ing Mountain" by Li Po, translated
by Sam Hamill, from *Crossing the Yellow River: Three Hundred Poems from
the Chinese* (Rochester, N.Y.: BOA Editions, 2000). Reprinted by
permission of the translator.
David Rice: Stanzas from "The First Petal" by Gail Sher and
David Rice. Copyright © by Gail Sher and David Rice.
Reprinted by permission.

Published in the United States by Bell Tower, an imprint of the
Crown Publishing Group, a division of Random House, Inc., New York.
www.crownpublishing.com

Bell Tower and colophon are registered trademarks of
Random House, Inc.

Library of Congress Cataloging-in-Publication Data
Sher, Gail
Writing the fire! : yoga and the art of making
your words come alive / Gail Sher.
Includes bibliographical references.
I. Authorship.   2. Authorship—Psychological aspects.
3. Yoga.   I. Title.
PN145.S466 2006
808'.02—dc22   2005024903

ISBN-13: 978-0-307-20991-7
ISBN-10: 0-307-20991-1

Printed in the United States of America

I   3   5   7   9   10   8   6   4   2

First Edition

For my beloved

BRENDAN

ACKNOWLEDGMENTS

It is with a sense of warmth and gratitude that I recognize the key individuals who have contributed to the emergence of this work:

Merry Benezra (for her vision, discernment, wit);

Brendan Collins (for his eye and heart and magnificent quiet mind);

Susan Weber (for the perfection of her knowledge, munificence, and gracious flexibility);

Marlene McCall at Creative Office Services (for guess what!);

Mark Horner (for the incentive of Shadow Yoga);

Martin Hunke (for deepening and honing yoga's secret profundities);

Adzom Paylo Rinpoche (for awakening within me the lurking truth of emptiness);

The Tibetan Buddhist *sangha* (who arouse and support the notion of vast empty space);

Nina Zolotow (for her amazing editing, patience, and swiftness);

Donald Moyer (for his inspired teaching/dedication/ willingness to help);

My ever-generous parents (who don't even know how much they help).

Special thanks to my editor, Toinette Lippe, and my agent, Sarah Jane Freymann, through whose effort Toinette (and consequently Bell Tower) entered the realm of this project.

CONTENTS

"PRACTICE, PRACTICE. ALL IS COMING!"

IMMERSION 1: CENTERING PRACTICE

IMMERSION 2: UNRAVELING PRACTICE

IMMERSION 3: ATTENDING PRACTICE

IMMERSION 4: RESISTANCE PRACTICE

IMMERSION 5:
ROOTING/REBOUNDING PRACTICE

IMMERSION 6: FLOWING PRACTICE

IMMERSION 7: ALIGNING PRACTICE

IMMERSION 8: RESTORATIVE PRACTICE

MOON DAYS

SECRET TEACHING OF THE WHITEST HORSE

SHE (THE WORD): TERMINOLOGY

FOREWORD

In *Writing the Fire!*, Gail Sher reveals how the practice of yoga can nourish and sustain your writing, and how the practice of writing—the art of arranging words in unexpected but revealing combinations—can inform and deepen your experience of yoga.

The idea of practice is central to this book. Practice is something we return to day after day without ever expecting to be finished. Practice involves repetition, performing the same pose on the same mat, or sitting at the same desk confronting the same blank page, wondering what will emerge today.

Practice is our intention to avoid the mechanical and the habitual, our commitment to seek what is fresh, spontaneous, and joyful in the same place we looked for it yesterday. In this sense, anything can become a practice—gardening, a relationship, or even standing in line at the bank—as long as we can maintain this commitment.

The practice of *hatha yoga* (the discipline of yoga poses, or *asanas,* and breathing techniques, or *pranayama*) is directly concerned with balancing and sustaining energy—both physical energy and psychic energy. In particular, yoga tradition defines three qualities of energy or being, known as the *gunas:* dynamic or active (*rajasic*); lethargic or inert (*tamasic*); and calm and alert (*sattvic*).

Anyone who has ever struggled with writing is aware of these three states. At one extreme is the overheated, or *rajasic*, state, when your brain is frenzied and your fingers on the keyboard can't keep pace with the hectic nature of your thoughts. The runaway mind is often self-induced, especially when there is a critical deadline to meet, but this overstimulation is ultimately self-defeating. Operating in a *rajasic* mode plays havoc with your nervous system and leaves you feeling exhausted.

At the other end of the spectrum is the sluggish, or *tamasic*, state, when you stare despondently at a few entrenched words that stubbornly refuse to convey your meaning, despite your heaving them back and forth from one part of your unfinished paragraph to another. The listless mind churns round and round without moving forward. In the *tamasic* state, progress is very slow.

The yogic ideal is the *sattvic* state, when your mind is calm and alert, poised between action and reflection, and your breath is soft and pervasive. When you write in the *sattvic* mode, you don't know whether your words come from your fingers or from your brain, your body and mind act in such harmony. Ideas form themselves with a natural logic and sentences appear on the page at a leisurely, sustainable pace. Your writing seems effortless.

As Gail Sher demonstrates so well, yoga practice can help you awaken, transform, and direct your creative energy as a writer. You can practice yoga for fifteen or twenty minutes before you begin writing to focus your attention. You can take a short *asana* break during a writing session to clear your head. You can follow a stressful period of writing with restful poses and gentle *pranayama* to restore your energy if you feel depleted. Best of all, you can include yoga in the very act of writing, by sitting upright at your desk with a balanced spine, being mindful of your breath.

In their dedication to practice, the yogi and the writer are both concerned with form. To achieve the fullest expression of their chosen form, they must not only love and respect the form, but also realize the limitations inherent in the form.

For the yogi, the form is the ideal shape of the pose. As a practitioner, you must accept your own limitations and discover the places of secret resistance before the essential nature of the pose is revealed to you. For the writer, the form may be a poem, a novel, a play, an instruction manual, or a journal. As a writer, you must consider what the form helps you to say easily and what it discourages you from saying, and then find a way to say that too.

Writing the Fire! encourages writers to approach their writing with the clarity and presence of yogis, and teaches yogis how to temper their awareness with the heat of words and images. As a poet-yogi, creative thinker, and writing mentor, Gail Sher celebrates the fullest expression of our being.

DONALD MOYER,
DIRECTOR OF THE YOGA ROOM,
BERKELEY, CALIFORNIA, AND AUTHOR OF
YOGA: AWAKENING THE INNER BODY

OPENING THE GATE

Unless freedom is gained in the body,
freedom of the mind is a far-fetched idea.

B. K. S. IYENGAR

GLIMPSING THE BUDDHA

That writing teaches writing is an incontrovertible truth. (One person cannot "teach" another how.) "So why do you represent yourself as a writing teacher?" a writer understandably asks. Because this is the best way I can help others cultivate the optimal conditions for making their writing happen.

Wherefore enters yoga. Yoga doesn't teach writing, but it is perhaps the most sophisticated, accessible, tried-and-true method of "inner disarmament" (to appropriate His Holiness the Dalai Lama's words. See below).

"Sophisticated?" you query. "What does that mean?"

When the Buddha elected to turn the Wheel of the *Dharma*, he faced the task of conveying the fruits of an inexplicable enlightenment experience to a wide variety of minds. Attuning himself to the spiritual development of each and every audience, his first turning was for those of beginning understanding, his second for intermediate and more advanced practitioners, and his third answered any leftover questions. In this way everyone's needs were satisfied.

Emulating the Buddha's impeccable pedagogy, we draw forth yoga, which easily adapts to specific (and very personal) situations. Its simplest techniques have profound repercussions. Dip anywhere into this vast legacy of wisdom and you will (if you are faithful and sincere) reap manifold positive benefits.

Since, as a writer, you are your own tool, what benefits you benefits your writing. Yoga is amazingly porous. Its principles and practices seamlessly morph into an aid that unearths the voice that is (and always has been) lurking in a writer's heart.

THE SKY IS IN OUR HEART

As I just mentioned, His Holiness the Dalai Lama suggests that "inner disarmament" is a universal way for opening the heart and mind.

But what *is* inner disarmament? And how does its wondrous space become ours?

One way is practice. Practice carves a passage to a sacred place of peace.

In beginning a practice, we want alertness and ease. Though intent on setting a routine, let it not be a plodding one. Instead, allow it to be vast. Out of vastness, joy arises.

As a species, we think WAY TOO SMALL. In terms of our potential, our basic nature, our telekinetic condition, our general idea is pitiful in comparison to the EXPANSIVE truth. And falsehood spreads. Pretty soon we're boxing ourselves in so routinely that we ourselves fail to see.

Writers need to see. The broader our vision, the clearer our focus. With perseverance our mind becomes more kind, our heart more steadfast, our speech more generous, our behavior more realized. The blessings we inevitably attract will rise and shine upon our writing.

THE TWO LIVES
OF YOGA

The Hindu story of Ananta, king of the Nagas (serpents), describes him carrying the treasures of the entire universe on his head whilst holding Lord Vishnu in the coils of his lap. This image is often used to illustrate the sutra of Patanjali (author of the *Yoga Sutra*, circa second century C.E.) that describes the essential qualities of yoga practice: *sthira sukha asanam*—alertness and relaxation—the double attributes needed simultaneously to hold the world and cradle the god Vishnu.

Sthira means "conscious," "steady," "firm," "stable." *Sukha* refers to the ability to remain comfortable and at ease, without pain or agitation. This aspect of yoga is fulfilled when we feel awake and unstressed during our practice.

Writing *asanas* (shapes the embodying of which similarly empower a writer) have the same dual requirements. To understand how we can best bring them forward, we must understand writing's anatomy and kinesiology.

Anatomy is about structure—how a writing posture stacks up. Kinesiology is about the mechanics of interior movement.

When a posture is cultivated properly, the body (our felt image of it) lengthens and widens. "Coinciding with the infinite," Patanjali says. When a posture is practiced correctly, the practitioner extends beyond the skin, merging with the sky.

Indeed, Patanjali describes relaxation as *asana*'s very essence. He uses the term *shaithilya*, which means "loosening" not merely the body, but opinions, concerns, hopes.

The mind is naturally free. Through various persistent attitudes, this spaciousness contracts. Actually, the mind never contracts. It is the illusion of contraction that yogis address.

As yoga unravels patterns, habits, obstructions, the mind's cycles are interrupted. Aware of its activity, the mind lets go and sinks.

For wholeness, we need to risk our entire being, which is dimensionless, unimaginable, uncompromised.

WRITING *ASANA*

*If a Prostitute Teaching a Parrot to
Sing the Name of God Becomes Illumined,
Then So Can Mirabai*

❧

Inayat Khan writes that the practice of Indian music is based on a culture of stimulating intuition, a feminine force that eludes language. It may be felt as a vibration (rather than a sound), like the overtones from a sitar.

When His Holiness the Dalai Lama speaks of "inner disarmament," he is whispering such overtones to you. Think of him as a translator, passing the vibrations of precious secrets on to one who sits at a crossroads.

The Tibetan symbol for *translator* is a two-headed bird. This bird both looks behind itself to its land of origin and forward to a new one. Thus it connects two worlds.

To appreciate, enjoy, and fully benefit from a primer that likewise draws from disparate worlds (writing and yoga), we, like this bird, must meld diverse symbols (integrate yoga's ancient ideology with—should we choose—the most contemporary urbanese).

Sit for a while contemplating the idea (its bearing on you personally) and allow your thoughts to drift into writing.

APOLOGIA

It has been brought to my attention that my writing style can be cryptic. In some cases, abrasively so. I tend to begin with the broad and proceed to the narrow. This allows the reader space to mold the concept to *her* mind. Some find this irritating. Where specificity limits, rather than liberates, I choose abstraction.

Thus a little explanation is required, first about the purpose of spareness and second about how a reader might best make use of this quality.

Regarding the former, "less is more" is called for when the reader thereby may derive a more personal (offbeat) meaning from the text. While it is true that I might think (and experience things) more abstractly (it seems anyway) than many, although the reader may have to struggle to tie up my loose ends, sometimes there is benefit in the effort. Though I've attempted to articulate this in the text with statements like "This is deliberately mind-boggling," there are occasions where a "large" concept is simply left to echo in the reader's heart— "on hold," so to speak.

If at first you feel confused, do not panic. Do not jump to

a negative judgment. If you fail to grasp a meaning, stop, open yourself to the mystery, then slowly enter it and wait. Tell yourself that you will simply record what arises at this moment (never mind the formal instruction).

Think of such places as opportunities to practice patience, the foremost writerly virtue. Usually there is no right or wrong. Usually there is room for your own unique understanding, over time, gradually to emerge.

Writing follows inner growth. Part of a writer's process is to watch and, like a fond mother, rejoice!

GUIDELINES TO
EASE YOUR WAY

1. Any of the writing *asanas* that do not come packaged with a prewriting *hatha yoga asana* can be mixed and matched with those that do. Each "immersion" is an energetic unit. Once you grasp its theme, the ordering is unimportant.

2. For those who just want to practice *asanas,* I've chosen not to unduly burden the text with theory. However, the final section of the book pertains to terminology. Though by no means exhaustive, it may help. Consult it whenever. (No need to save it for last.)

3. While both yoga and writing are endeavors of profound magnitude, their precision is one of integrity, aesthetics, philosophy (i.e., emotional, psychological, spiritual) rather than scientific. The craft of writing does indeed have its demanding side, but its demands are not the same as a physicist's. Instructions are cues. If you register them mentally, this is sufficient.

4. Chapter titles (ideally) intrigue. Please take pleasure in them. If you do not grasp the connection between a title and what follows, bide awhile, relax into the words, and allow a marriage to develop. Whatever coupling serves *you* is the correct one.

5. Sanskrit or no Sanskrit? Sanskrit terms are sprinkled throughout the text, along with their translation (which you can also find in the glossary). They might have been omitted. But, however obliquely, they convey yoga's ancient mind and world. If they bother you, please skip them. Their presence alone will seep into your consciousness and perhaps one day may be a help.

6. Regarding quotations, I apologize. I am an avid reader and many concepts pass through my mind. While I recall their lessons, I sometimes forget their source. "Well, this is not a scholarly text," I tell myself, ineffectively assuaging my guilt. While many of my quotations will lack specific origins, my choice, nonetheless, is to share them.

7. Above all, remember: Yoga is primarily a movement from one point to another, higher one, previously beyond reach. What (am I doing), how (do I keep doing it), where (am I in my process), and why (for God's sake) are constantly evolving questions whose constantly evolving answers thrust the writer into an ever-broadening sphere of self-reflection and pause. By superimposing yoga's wisdom heritage onto the transformational process of opening the heart and mind, *Writing the Fire!* offers a Way for a writer, in her whirling evolutionary process, to stay centered.

MAY WE ALL BOW
TO SLOWNESS

While individuals vary, the natural pace of human beings is slow. In an atmosphere of slowness, kindness and thoughtfulness flourish. Writers need to be kind and thoughtful. Because they need to be authentic. (Kind and thoughtful is the way we naturally are.)

Hurry (pressure) makes one slightly insane. It *will* impact your writing because it impacts your central nervous system.

Being peace is the best way to demonstrate it. Being slow is a beginning. You cannot be violent to yourself (rush) and expect your writing ultimately to meet your standards.

Being slow is a teacher. It will remind you of your standards while helping you to implement them.

Being slow is a friend.

VENTURING INTO THE YOGI-WRITER'S WAY

We of the Occident are about to arrive at a
crossroads that was reached by the thinkers of
India some seven hundred years before Christ.

HEINRICH ZIMMER

PATH OF RETURN

Yoga (the word) derives from the Sanskrit *yuj* (to yoke or harness). Etymologically speaking, *yoga* refers both to the *endeavor* to achieve union and to the *state* of union itself. "Union of *what?*" you might wonder.

Conscious subject and mental object, say the earliest texts. It means your mind (the observer) merges with an external object (the observed). Such merging is a process that includes

1. Suspending disbelief (allowing for the possibility—and benefits—of achieving it)

2. Purifying oneself of the residue of past unskillful behaviors

3. Gaining merit

4. Contemplating the meaning of such a union

5. Eventually, by thoroughly penetrating the concept with one's mind, directly experiencing it

Their merging is called *samadhi* (literally, "placing" or "putting together"; see "Straightening the Ground," p. 178). *Yoga* (or *samadhi*) is thus *both* the technology and the state of self-transcendence.

THE JUICE OF *DHARMA*
HAS ONE TASTE

The Sanskrit word *smriti* (mindfulness) literally means "re-membering." Re-membering (re-collecting) or, as in yoga, re-uniting all our disparate parts, happens when we pay attention.

Mindfulness is a capacity. Breath, posture, movement, feeling, thought, and the phenomena around us all comprise its web of interrelationship.

We are always giving our attention to something. The giving may be appropriate (as when we are paying full attention to the present moment) or inappropriate (as when we are attentive to something that pulls us away).

In the *Bhaddekaratta Sutta* the Buddha taught: "Looking deeply at life as it is/in the very here and now,/the practitioner dwells/in stability and freedom." As Patanjali defines *asana*—that posture which is stable and easeful—dwelling in the here and now = YOGA.

YOGA'S TREE:
ITS EIGHT LIMBS

The **root** of the tree is the *yamas* (the outer observances). Since these "organs of action" control the "organs of perception and the mind," yogis think of *yamas* as the foundation.

The **trunk** of the tree are the *niyamas* (the inner observances). These control the organs of perception—eyes, ears, nose, tongue, and skin.

The tree's **branches** flare in various shapes and directions. These are the *asanas,* the postures that align physical functions with psychological patterns.

From the branches grow **leaves** whose interaction with air supplies the tree with energy. They correspond to *pranayama,* the science of breath.

The branches of the tree are protected by **bark,** which also protects the tree's insides. Bark corresponds to *pratyahara,* the interiorizing of the senses.

The **sap** of the tree, the juice that carries the energy, represents *dharana* (concentration).

Flowers bloom when the tree is healthy. Like meditation (*dhyana*) their nature is freshness.

The **fruit** is *samadhi*. "As the essence of the tree is in the fruit, so the essence of the practice of yoga is in the freedom, poise, peace, and beatitude of *samadhi*, where the body, the mind, and the soul are united and merge with the Universal Spirit," states B. K. S. Iyengar.

ASHTANGA[1] YOGA
FOR WRITERS

Sometimes the five *yamas* (outer precepts) and five *niyamas* (inner precepts) are referred to as "restraints." More accurately they are declarations of our inherent nature. Since as writers, our inherent nature is at once our origin, tool, and product, if you abide by these basic writing ethics, your writing will unfold by itself.

THE FIVE *YAMAS* OF WRITING

Ahimsa (Not-Harming)
Writers write. Our vow is to be present for it. Anything that interferes is harmful. Thus we avoid such circumstances and behaviors.

Satya (Truthfulness)
Honesty in word and action is a guiding principle that most adults accept. The hard part is knowing what that is. As writers we're given drafts to try out our truth. Certainty = mastery.

Asteya (Not-Stealing)

Writers may steal if they turn what they steal into something entirely original. If they pull from the universe what appeals to them to pull, then reshape it. Meticulously. (It's a cosmic law.)

Brahmacarya (Regulation of Sexual Energy)[2]

Writing is so hard that we must bring to it all of our resources. Including sexual resources. Sexual energy is energy. Writers need it for their writing.

For one person this may mean abstinence. For another it might mean frequent, passionate sex. You need to know what keeps you taut. And follow what you know. (No labels.)

Aparigraha (Not-Grasping)

Grasping is aggressive. Chögyam Trungpa Rinpoche was quite clear: Fine art never arises from an aggressive state of mind.

THE FIVE *NIYAMAS* OF WRITING

Shauca (Purity)

Since this is the surest way to live life at a higher resolution (with more clarity and happiness), it perforce is the Way for a writer. What does purity mean to you?

Santosha (Contentment)

Practicing contentment helps a writer stay present. Whereby her writing becomes alive, sparkling, vivid.

Tapas (Fire)

Inner heat is a writer's route to keeping herself stoked. She might live on the edge financially, emotionally, physically. Or brace herself by a schedule, which provides a wall for her artistic back. Good writing originates from "alert and ready."

Svadhyaya (Self-Study)

Svadhyaya literally means "one's own" (*sva*) + "going into" (*adhyaya*). The more accurately a writer articulates the subtlety of *that*, the more sharply will she pierce the living nerve of the human heart.

Ishvara Pranidhana (Devotion to God)

The best expression of devotion is skillful behavior. Dedicating your efforts protects them from ill effects and allows you to steer their benefits. If you make a dedication immediately following your writing period, its merit will not be lost.

ASANA

The Indian yoga researcher M. V. Bhole characterized *asanas* as "molds," "casts," or "patterns" because "they are to be main-tained for a certain length of time in a passive manner with an emphasis to achieve relaxation of those muscles involved in assuming the posture itself."[3] As such the postures become psychophysical templates promoting symmetry, balance, and harmony, as well as inner peace. A writing *asana* is the same.

PRANAYAMA
(CONTROL OF THE LIFE FORCE)

Writers must have control of their energy (life force) so that they can literally wrap their life around writing. All the talent in the world will do nothing for a writer who cannot get herself to her desk.

PRATYAHARA (SENSE WITHDRAWAL)

The sheer skill to redirect the senses inward toward their source is critical for a writer's expression of intelligence, wit, and kindness.

DHARANA (CONCENTRATION)

Forget life stages as in childhood, adolescent, adult, old age. Think rather of "before learning concentration," "after learning concentration," "after learning deep concentration," and "after learning concentration deep enough to realize the inherent emptiness of existence."

DHYANA (MEDITATION)

The depth of absorption of a writer's mind = the quality of her writing.

SAMADHI
(PURE ESSENCE OF ALL THAT EXISTS)

The peace, joy, and equanimity that come from regular writing practice.

WRITING *ASANA*

Before Writing Is the "Thought of Writing"

Sometimes, before we are ready for a task (or have even claimed it as our own) we find ourselves preparing. A writer-to-be might notice herself, for example, endlessly scavenging office supply stores. By the time it dawns on her that she would like to write (regularly and with intention), materially speaking, she's ready. In the same way, writers inadvertently collect books, quotations, inspiring thoughts, and WORDS.

Consider your words. Select those that you prize, learned under unusual circumstances, or perhaps have long mistaken. Tell the story of your favorite ones. Nonwords are also permissible if they are meaningful to you in some way.

BEFORE YOU PRACTICE

Create a writing temple.

The doing of an activity supports its continued doing. Make it easy on yourself. Create a space for your writing to happen.

Clean, quiet, neat. Surround yourself with what nourishes you. Your main tool is your concentration.

Which you want to build. Posture helps. To support your concentration, choose a chair that encourages a straight spine.[4]

Writers don't need much.

TAKE FROM YOUR POSE
PRECISELY WHAT
YOU CAN USE AND
NO MORE. DISCOVER
WHAT THAT IS.

Writing is a process. It happens over time. Increment by precious increment.

Please enjoy the process. (There's no hurry. Once you are engaged in it, you're already "there.")

Thus, the task, each day, will be dependent on that day's circumstances. Skill for a writer in part implies that when she arrives at her desk, she will, with greater and greater certainty, know what "today's task" is.

And when she's completed it, she stops. "Enough is enough," as my seventy-five-year-old grandmother once said.

Knowing when to stop, when to simply "lay it aside for now" is a tremendous liberator. It is good in the beginning. It is good in the middle (especially if you've chosen the wrong path). And it's excellent at the end (so as not to overstay/overstate/exaggerate/go on and on).

VAST OCEANS OF TIME

Time feels short, but we have "infinite time, infinite incarnations," Robert Thurman says. Or, time feels long. We think we have many years to accomplish what we want, but suddenly, one day we wake up . . .

The former is predicated on an understanding of the mind as a continuum over the course of many lifetimes. The latter (whose prime directive is the unknown date of death) pushes for action NOW so as not to take this life (or the propitious nature of future ones) for granted.

For writers, the best attitude is a mixture. Rushing doesn't work. It curtails the plumbing of one's full experience from whence (our priceless) clarity is derived. Dallying doesn't either. Instead, holding the thought of death at the forefront of our consciousness, we immerse ourselves in the task at hand. For writers, this means writing, regularly if not daily, with a mind as open as the sky. With a mind that will NEVER die. If we are holding the thought of death in a prominent enough place, we can think this way.

Vast time yields vast space. (Time and space are sisters.)

Imagine a landscape whose boundaries disappear—for example, the Tibetan high plateau, the Grand Canyon, fields of wheat, a huge body of water. If we incorporate such perspectives into our mind stream, and visit them when we write, the correct viewpoint arises on its own.

WRITING *ISN'T* TALKING
(THEY HAVE SEPARATE LINES
OF DEVELOPMENT)

In America it's hard. Many struggle with the basics of English. Getting those basics onto paper *is* the "written language," but it's not *writing*, the craft, which communicates multidimensionally.

Talking has a commensurate craft. As does lecturing, socializing, horsing around. A person may excel in one or all of these and not be a writer.

Writing can turn into talking inside the reader's head. You read something, mull it over (for example, repeat it to yourself). It's a way of slowing down.

WRITING IS
A STATE OF BEING

Often (until there has been a deep and heartfelt transformation) when we simply "do what we do," we're repeating habitual behaviors. Moving calmly allows the mind to notice.

Probably as you approach your desk you are thinking about WHAT. WHAT AM I GOING TO WRITE? Instead, sit down, gather yourself, offer up your efforts, and, by way of ritual, write the date. Write methodically, forming each letter. As you make the *u* in *June,* become so immersed in its undulations that you forget for a moment that this shape is part of anything (like another letter) that may precede or follow.

Note the weight and volume of your arm, the changes in your breath, the shifts in your mental perceptions, the altering quality of your mind, and the fluctuation in your attitude.

If you pause to find your center before beginning to write, you may find yourself writing about your real subject NOW, instead of what you thought your subject was or planned to take as your subject, neither of which would be as compelling.

If you slow down (establish yourself in your *hara*) your content will effervesce.

WRITING IS AN OFFERING

Writing is an offering. To preserve its purity, you must prepare and protect the context from which it is generated. Context = when, where, how, how long, why.

WHEN, for a writer, is his readiness. Probably you know. Probably you are aware of the rhythms of your energy, its qualities and seasons, daily peaks and lulls. (Early morning, late afternoon, the quiet of night are all good possibilities.)

WHERE is his space. Which should be clean. But we don't just clean the space. We clean our minds. While you are physically scrubbing the floor, mentally you are cleaning anger, attachment, jealousy.

HOW is purity of spirit. Check your motivation—that it is unsullied (not driven by self-centered desires). You might repeat an affirmation or make an offering. Flowers, stones, or fruit can be a way of opening the heart.

HOW LONG should be determined beforehand. When the allotted time is up, stop. This will instill a desire to continue. Overstaying can set up false expectations (unfavorable tendencies in future sessions).

WHY is because. Writers write. It's their first noble truth.

FROM THE
BEGINNINGLESS

According to ancient texts[5] the physical body, an outer shell or casing, is animated by an inner, energy body. Both bodies are made of energy, but the former, like molten lava hardened into rock, has lost the fluidity, warmth, and luster that characterize the latter.

How to integrate the body of light (the body's internal intelligence) with the outer physical body is the study of a writer.

Often the body of light is locked within the physical body. While it unceasingly gives life, we are not always aware that it is doing so. Awareness, however, lures it from captivity. Awareness is cultivated by balancing and rebalancing five opposite poles.

UNDOING THE BODY, UNDOING THE MIND

Physical tension is an activity. A doing. Some of it is conscious. Undoing the body frees the attention which relaxes back from the surface and falls into a deeper place.

DONA HOLLEMAN, YOGI

Undoing is the ability to find neutral. Think of muddy water. When you first extract it from a pond, it is suffused with muck. If you set it down, after a few minutes, the floating debris will sink toward the bottom. This sediment collects, forming a layer of dirt separate from the now-clearer upper portion. While the slightest movement might upset this balance, returning the glass to rest quickly restores it.

The mind is the same. A writer's job is to familiarize herself with the particular cues that her mind provides when a concept (or feeling) is still murky and needs settling. "Neutral" means trusting her ability to find the antidotes that facilitate the emergence of her mind's natural clarity.

INTENDING / DREAMING

The more clearly you can visualize a picture of what you want to perform, the more the result will fulfill your expectation.

Intention jump-starts the process. It moves the body faster than the mind. Just as all our postures are already imprinted in our bodies, so is all our writing.

Reading triggers remembering. Dreaming also. Once a yogi dreamed he was doing a pose he couldn't do. The next day he could do it.

So find the balance between conscious intent and unconscious dreaming. Write from there.

> *The body should always move in opposite directions simultaneously to gain maximum space and ease in the joints.*

DONA HOLLEMAN

Gravity provides a reference point (a stable direction). Rooting (mentally dropping into the earth) makes this directive more alive.

As the rebound sails upward, it expands from the inside. (The more you release down, the more the potential to bounce back up.) Lightness and buoyancy will manifest in your writing.

Take a nugget of pain. If you inch your way toward its interior, excavating, examining, deciphering its terrain, afterward you will feel cleaner, freer, purer, as if a tether has been cut. It *has*, emotionally and psychologically. Since inspiration can be the result, writers need to cultivate, mine, and craft such opportunities.

CONNECTING/BREATHING

Rebound requires connection. The farther reaches of the body-mind stay in relation to one another through alignment, consciousness, and breath.

Human beings have internal relay stations. Energy accumulates in one, then is batonned to the next. As a writer, you need to know these "innermost" landmarks.

Energetically they can be your *cakras* (see "Lining Up the *Cakras*," p. 200), emotionally they may take the form of feelings, and philosophically the form of thoughts, each progressive level of which serves your liberation. Historically they may form a life collage. And creatively? (Please notice and fill in the blank.)

The body-mind is elastic (not frozen). Knots (stuck points) are places where the connection is broken.

Breath is fuel. It powers the mind. Without breath, writing looks hollow, flat, depressed. Breath encourages flushed, pink cheeks.

Prana (the life force in breath) is a direct link to the body of light. Inhale means unconditional receiving. Exhale, unconditional giving. When breath is moving fully in the body, we feel, through the skin, our contact with the universe. (See "Prewriting and Writing *Asanas:* Vital Breaths," p. 158.)

ELONGATING / RIDING THE FLOW

Stretching is the mechanical lengthening of one muscle by shortening another. There is a limit beyond which the muscle will rip (when the contractions of the shortening muscle exceed the capacity of the lengthening muscle to expand).

Elongating is entirely different. Deep within the fibers of a muscle is a hidden door. It is opened by breathing and once opened, it allows the muscles to undo themselves. Both lengthening and shortening muscles undo and ride the energy flow. There's no danger, fatigue, or residue.

The process of elongating comes about by rooting, connecting, and breathing in which breath is the link as well as fuel that pulls the body-mind along.

In elongating, the muscle relinquishes its effort to do. Then it extends. Other body parts pick up on the impulse and let go too.

When the mind in turn lets go, writing flows freely.

ENGAGING THE SHADOW

"What's *that?*" you might ask. (It's a kinder way of saying that you really don't think you have a shadow.)

Probably, if you've attempted ongoing regular writing periods, you have met with . . . limitations, frustrations, difficulties, uncomfortable situations. But what are *these?* They are *you* (from another point of view).

If, toward dusk, as you're walking down the street, your eyes fall to the ground, off to the side you might notice a silhouette. It is definitely connected with you. In fact, you can't shake it off. (It's the ghost of what bothers you in your writing periods.)

For inside an area of displeasure is an odd form of you.

The *Shiva Samhita* describes a daily ritual in which the yogi looks steadily at his own shadow and then looks up at the sky. One day he sees his own divine reflection. It's called the "invocation of the shadow man."

Because the shadow (in this context) *is* the body of light, the shape and attributes of one's shadow reveal a lot about how one unconsciously *blocks* light.

The Yogi does not cause the transformation of nature, he merely removes the obstacles to its flow just as the farmer lifts the sluice gates to irrigate the rice fields.

YOGA SUTRA

As the body of light's shadow drifts, it releases energy, which carries heat and fluidity. Writers must locate and harness it for their writing. *This* is the "invocation."

We *dance* the body of light when the physical vehicle surfs the energetic one—when the passageways connecting the two are aligned and open. Writing from *here* (from the body's innate intelligence) there is no fatigue (or even effort) but, rather, an increased sense of joy. The body-mind reaches and reconnects, not only within (its internal parts to each other) but without (to the surrounding sky). Thus lies the beauty, power, and grace beholden to the yogi-writer's spirit.

Insight, says the *Yoga Sutra,* is a fiery shining river flowing continuously in the mind. Its signposts on the body's surface are called *marmas* (vital junctions). *Marmas* act as the river's springs, through which the writer learns to connect to her energy currents and pathways.

Most important is the navel. It is not just a matter of centering or developing core strength, but of learning to trust "gut feelings." The theory of vital junctions and inner pathways comes to life through the navel, not the head.

The presence of the shadow body emerges with the deepening of practice. If you mentally visualize it, one day it will simply arise. Trying doesn't help. It is better to relax into your routine, still the mind, and trust the energies that ripple through the shadow's layers to circulate as they will.

"Lift your shadow body first. Allow it to raise your physical body!" hummed Dona Holleman softly, guiding her *asana* class out of Triangle Pose. "How does one do that?" one thinks. But by loosening the mind (*allowing* her instruction), it is done!

DEDICATION MAGNIFIES THE BENEFITS OF POSITIVE ACTIONS AND PREVENTS THEM FROM BEING LOST

For writers, prayer focuses intention. Two points in our daily practice benefit. At the beginning, being mindful that our motivation is pure, we offer our efforts up. Then, when our practice is complete, we dedicate the merit we have generated.

Offering and dedication weigh in slightly differently. After a writer is seated with a comfortable, straight spine and before she begins to write, she consciously aligns her energies and then gives everything away. "Here's my best. Take it all!" is the feeling.

At the conclusion of her practice, she dedicates the positive energy she has accumulated toward a specific result. Like a horse, accumulated positive energy will carry her in whatever direction she determines. A writer seizes this opportunity.

Because once dedicated, the benefit remains. One drop of water quickly evaporates. Dedication secures that drop in the ocean.

By intentionally inhabiting her efforts—immersing herself and then sealing the immersion with prayer—a writer partakes, as Zen master Hakuin says, in the elixir of "verbal *prajna.*"

YOGA PROPS,
YOGA CLOTHES

❦

Props first. Props allow you to achieve a more natural alignment. Being more fully immersed in a posture makes it easier to attend to its subtler aspects. A prop can help you stretch, opening different parts of your body. As you experiment, ask yourself: How does this prop (or lack of it) affect my body, mind, emotions?

The following is a list of props that might enhance your experience of the *hatha yoga asanas* in this book. All are optional.

YOGA MAT

A thin (one-eighth of an inch thick), sticky rectangular rubber mat approximately 24 by 68 inches, used primarily to prevent slipping. If you don't have one, you can use the floor (if you're careful of your bones and don't get too cold) or carpet (provided it is not spongy).

YOGA BLOCK

Made of wood, cork, or foam, 4 by 6 by 9 inches, to build a solid raised surface on which you can sit or rest your hands or fingers.

YOGA STRAP

A cotton belt with a buckle, 1½ inches by 6 feet, that allows you to reach a part of your body that you cannot reach with ease.

PROBABLY TWO BLANKETS

Several single-size cotton or woolen blankets, approximately 62 by 80 inches (usually folded into a rectangle), to furnish a *firm* raised surface on which you can sit or over which you can drape your body.

ROUND BOLSTER

A specially designed firm cylindrical pillow over which you can drape your body.

FLAT BOLSTER

A specially designed firm rectangular pillow on which to prop your body or over which to drape it. (Flat and round bolsters have different optimal purposes.)

EYE PILLOW

A small rectangular cloth bag filled with flax seeds, approximately 1 by 4 by 8½ inches, to relax your eyes and face during rest or restorative poses.

NOTEPAD AND PENCIL

As you practice you may have thoughts, which, if you write them down, will cease to distract you.

SANDBAG

A large rectangular bag made from densely woven fabric filled with ten pounds of sterilized sand, used to anchor a part of the body or provide deep tension-releasing pressure.

FOLDING CHAIR

Choose a chair that is sturdy (with nonslip feet) to ease difficult postures and for specific stretches. It should have an opening below the part that supports the upper back that is large enough to accommodate your hips.

CLOTHES

While comfortable, loose clothing is heavenly and perfect for writing *asanas*, for prewriting *hatha yoga asanas*, "loose" isn't always "comfortable." Baggy fabric can bunch, get in your way, slide down your body, fall into your face. It's better, taking your climate and body type into account, to wear as little as possible and layer. For example, you might want the option, all in the same practice session, to wear leggings, a tank top, a long-sleeved T-shirt, a sweater, and/or a fleece. Keep them handy so that you can continually calibrate your body heat.

"PRACTICE, PRACTICE.
ALL IS COMING!"[6]

Yoga must be known through Yoga.

VYASA

A FORMLESS FIELD
OF BENEFACTION

Whenever you "take your seat," in meditation or in writing, you are practicing yoga!

Though literally translated as "comfortable seat," the word *asana* means to relax into the consciousness of life as it manifests through a shape. "Take your seat" thus means intention and the grace that follows deliberateness.

A synonym for *asana* is *pitha* ("shrine," "seat," or "sacred place"). Indeed, *asana* is a bow to one's body-mind as a divine temple. "Is my state of mind ready to host subtle energies and refined sounds?" a writer might pause to consider.

To allow an *asana* to transform us, we must immerse ourselves in its inner impulse. Skill = digesting and transmuting the particular vibrations of its power.

Which involves:

I. Standing aside. Observing the body-mind from a completely objective viewpoint.

2. Dialoguing with the inevitable tension that arises when we bump into unyielding places of old pain.

3. Palpating this tension with breath. Free-associate. Try to uncover its core.

4. Clarifying our ground, i.e., finding the dynamic balance for the animating movement of *prana*.

5. Redirecting our awareness to stillness.

WRITING ASANA

When All My Selves Throb Like a Trombone,
I Begin with an Urge

How does one begin? How does one begin anything? Let's ask Ganesha, the potbellied, elephant-headed god of writers, scribe of yoga, guardian of sacred spaces *and* of auspicious beginnings.

> Often I just listen—to the voice of my ancestors,
>   the hush of the sea, the wind when it was sun,
>   the desert's parched sigh.
> As my ears whip the air, I simply follow my nature.
> My ways are wily. Don't think you understand.
>   (I might jump-start via obstacles.)
> Like a bolt of thunder, sometimes I just begin.

How do *you* begin? Think about it. Connect with your typical state of mind as you enter a prospective (daunting) task.

Write the history of that state of mind. What is your first memory of it? Or, alternately, step inside and draft its autobiography.

THE ART OF
SEQUENCING

An *asana* is plump with virtues. Assuming its shape is beneficial. Assuming its shape with comfort, alertness, and ease munificently enhances its advantages. Juxtaposing one *asana* with others that have synergistic forces makes the original *asana* all the more useful. Sequencing (*vinyasa*—the word traditionally describes a linked series of *hatha yoga asanas*) is the art of masterfully minded juxtaposition.

The real *vinyasa* is the intention with which you practice.

Writing sequences build, integrate, and distribute different qualities of energy, of which there are three: *sattva*, wisdom; *rajas*, action; *tamas*, inertia. *Tamasic* energy is slow, lethargic, sluggish. *Rajasic* is dynamic and forceful. *Sattvic* energy is calm, clear, balanced, poised. (See "The Three *Gunas*," p. 192.)

Writers select and practice writing *asanas* to align their minds (meld them) with their bottom voice.

The presiding rule is restraint (passion controlled by form).

It works like a dam. Once your energy is harnessed, you direct it as you will. Sequencing, by superimposing a form on a series of events, almost does the whole job for you!

BE HERE NOW

If you wear an *asana* today the same way you wore it yesterday, you will notice that it no longer fits.

"That's obvious," you may think, drifting off into your thoughts. But since the body and mind work separately . . .

We need to challenge ourselves, work right at our edge, but not so far beyond it that we topple over.

For example, if you panic (*asanas* can be scary), how much are you likely to benefit? Better to back off and deal with the panic. Panic is intelligent. If it's there, *it* becomes your teacher.

THE AFTERLIFE
OF A POSE

"Today I'm going to do Mountain Pose," you say to yourself when you get up. You go to your spot. You have an idea in your mind of what this rooted, centered, standing position looks like. You align your feet, ankles, knees, thighs, pelvis, shoulders, ears. You're aware of your spine straightening, lengthening, becoming supple. Your breath slows down, hands relax, jaw drops. Pretty soon you forget that you're in a posture.

Later, in headstand, your body says, "Hey! This is Mountain Pose." The imprint of your previous work courses through your spine. Your tailbone drops, your thighs internally rotate, elongating and firming the plumb line.

Later, by the elevator, there you are in Mountain Pose without having even intended it!

Poses have an afterlife. You take one on. Later it takes on you.

Doing yoga itself may be part of yoga's afterlife. The shapes have a way of feeling so familiar. Sometimes your body simply knows, though to your recollection you've never seen this pose before.

Probably you, in a different shape, assumed this shape over and over and over.

Writing is like this. We spiral through our practice barely aware of precisely which shape we're refurbishing with air. The legacy of one shape is lugubrious. We eke it out word by word. "Whence this patch of slick, clear ice?" we wonder as we suddenly whiz past the blowing trees.

IMMERSION I: CENTERING PRACTICE

Moving Toward Balance

Before you assume a standing pose, while you are settling in your feet, sensing your roots, grounding your lower body, it's good to tilt forward, then backward, then to both sides. When you return to center, you are clearer about where that is. By taking ourselves "off" balance, it's easier to detect what's "on."

ONE DOESN'T DO YOGA; RATHER, ONE *IS* YOGA OR *IS IN* YOGA OR ONE IS NOT

❦

All he needs to do is stand beside you and you feel his adjustment.

STUDENTS OF SRI PATTABHI JOIS

It is a common principle—in psychotherapy, in weight training—that growth takes place in rest. It is between sessions that the real change occurs. To learn, we need to integrate, play, build courage to reside in the unknown. Which takes time, leisure, privacy.

Any writing program—indeed any program deeply rooted in one's psyche and personal history—must provide a place for first discovering how to tailor the practices to one's personal rhythms, routines, proclivities, strengths. The elements that are investigated in this series of immersions—unraveling, attending, resisting (working with obstacles), rooting and rebounding, flowing, alignment, and breath awareness—are all predicated on an understanding of balance.

Being balanced doesn't mean never being thrown off.

Rather, it means resilience—responding effectively to challenge.

Centering practice, designed for students to draw from their intuition (their body of light's intelligence), offers a structured context in which to explore the meaning of this dynamic in their writing.

PREWRITING *ASANA*

Body Scan

Start this exercise by sitting or lying comfortably, closing your eyes, and taking several long, deep breaths. Allow your body-mind to settle.

Bring your attention to the top of your head and feel the sensations there. Then, moving your attention downward, feel the sensations on the back and either side of your head, your ears, forehead, eyes, nose, cheeks, mouth, and jaw. Take your time. Be as slow and thorough as you like.

Continuing the scan, be careful not to use your eyes to direct your mind. This creates tension. Rather, connect directly with your sensations by feeling the body from the inside. In certain parts, it is common to feel numbness or even nothing. Mentally massage those areas.

You may find that as your consciousness deepens, images or thoughts arise. Allow them to pass and gently return to the sensations. *Intend* releasing all ideas, celebrating your physical aliveness.

Now begin a gradual and full review of the rest of your body. Starting with your neck and throat, move to your shoulders and slowly down your arms to your hands. Feel each finger—the palms, the backs of the hands—noticing tingling, pulsing, pressure, temperature.

Proceed to the sensations in your chest, upper back, shoulder blades, then down to the middle back, lower back, and abdomen. Feeling from within, what arises in your hips, buttocks, genitals, legs, feet, toes? Notice the pressure of contact and concomitant warmth or cold when your body touches the chair, cushion, or floor.

Now expand your awareness to include your entire body. Can you sense the subtle energy that gives life to every cell? Is there any center or boundary? What or who is abiding?

When you feel ready, slowly open your eyes and return your attention to the outside world.

PREWRITING AND WRITING *ASANA*

Happy Baby Pose

Think of a gurgling six-month-old rolling around, fiddling with its toes. Its flesh is soft, limbs supple. What is its facial expression?

Lie on your back with your feet up in the air and directly over your knees, and grip the outsides of your feet with your hands (or with a strap if you can't reach your feet).

Melt your back into the floor and rock your spine from side to side. As you release your hips, feel your sacrum spread. Your spine—from tailbone to skull—should undulate with each fully relaxed breath.

Now, go to your desk and write a story or poem from a baby's point of view.

PREWRITING AND WRITING *ASANA*

Cat Pose

Pretend you're a cat (get into the mind-set). Physically you're on your hands and knees, standing on four limbs. Each vertebra is floating. Your back reaches toward your tailbone, your chest toward your head. Feel the ripple of your breath pulsate through your spine in one prolonged wave.

As you press your shins downward, lengthen and deepen your groin to raise your sitting bones. Your lower back will arch. Your chest, neck, and head will rise skyward.

Now drop your tailbone between your legs, curl your head down, and hunch your back. Press your straight arms strongly into the floor. Tuck your chest into the crevice of your neck.

As a cat, what just happened? Write about your concerns, as if you were inhabiting the world as this animal.

PREWRITING AND WRITING *ASANA*

Lion Pose

Sit on your heels with your hands on your knees. Consciously lift your chest (as if you were a roaring lion), initiating the lift from your tailbone. The side walls of your chest should thrust forward and upward between your arms.

Firmly gaze at the tip of your nose, letting your eyes cross, and stick out your tongue as far as you can. Open your mouth WIDE and roar LOUDLY. Close your mouth, inhale through your nose, and roar again from the depths of your belly. The emptier you are, the farther your voice will project.

Transmute the intensity of the pose into words. Write on a subject of your choice with passion. (Lions aren't embarrassed.)

PREWRITING AND
WRITING *ASANA*

Volcano Pose

This pose is about staying connected—feet with mind, mind with feet.

Standing with your feet together, raise your arms directly over your head, allowing your body to receive the slight back bend that naturally occurs. Drop your shoulder blades down your back as you lift your arms farther behind your ears. Lengthen your waist, experiencing your evenly suspended ribs as your arms stretch upward.

Consciously draw the energy of the earth up through your body and out through your fingertips. Support the position with your chest. Keep your neck soft as you maximize the wideness of the muscles of your back without hardening or locking.

Can you grow another inch? Some people will pause and place a block between their hands to make even more vivid the solidity of this sinuous expansion.

Write about a time when you held up the sky.

WRITING *ASANA*

Balance the Fluid in Your Inner Ears

Once there was an author who was sued for libel. While the opposing lawyer exaggerated the offensiveness of certain quotations, the jury ruled that though two of the five were false and one defamatory, none had been written so recklessly as to constitute libel!

Write the piece for which the author was sued.

Note: As the title of the *asana* suggests, this exercise is intentionally mind-boggling. What happens when you are befuddled? How might you gently take care of yourself—that is, remain centered in your breath?

WRITING *ASANA*

When a Pickpocket Meets a Saint
All He Sees Are Her Pockets

Cadence—the balanced rhythmic flow of a writer's voice—mirrors the texture of her consciousness. For some (Gertrude Stein, Henry James, James Joyce) it would be impossible, without falsification, to extricate their meaning from the cadence with which they express it.

Compose a passage whose cadence rings the essence of your heart and mind. (Remember how you felt in Cat Pose or Happy Baby Pose, for example.)

WRITING *ASANA*

Teaching Isn't Given, It's Realized

❧

Often before a momentous occasion, the unconscious gathers itself in response. The universal surge cannot be stopped. Collective forces culminate in a singular sweep of energy. Everything is affected, including one's dreams.

Compose three dreams and follow with a commentary to "unpack" the buildup of tension and complexity. Are you able, having been thrown off by momentousness, to reestablish your balance?

Note: It might help first to imagine a specific occasion to which the three dreams are a prelude.

IMMERSION 2: UNRAVELING PRACTICE

When in Doubt, Relax!

There is a way of doing yoga poses that we call
asanas without the slightest effort.

VANDA SCARAVELLI, *AWAKENING THE SPINE*

DOING-WITHOUT-DOING

In Taoist literature there is a concept, *wei-wu-wei* (doing-without-doing). Doing belongs to the ego. Underlying the ego is the intelligence of the body. When the mind and ego are made quiescent through *wei-wu-wei,* this body intelligence takes over.

Wei-wu-wei encompasses a threefold process: first there is a conscious wish to achieve something; second a lull during which one stops worrying about the outcome; third (in the vacuum) the body's deeper intelligence takes over, "fulfilling" the wish.

Learning to invite the energy body—the body of light (which is usually latent)—to emerge and take the lead is the *art* of the yogi-writer.

In the initial unraveling practice, the mind crawls inside and notices: tension, blockages, stiffness. Being warmly observed, the body will, by itself, unfurl, like a tightly closed leaf.

Even the skin becomes translucent. By clarifying the skin (so that it no longer obstructs the free exchange of energy) we reconnect with surrounding space. Suddenly the world from which we write not only becomes bigger, it becomes quiet and one-pointed.

For writers, to start from where we are (and not a step or two ahead), first we step back, unwind a bit. *Then*, going forward, we're sure to be present.

PREWRITING *ASANA*

Three-Stepped Savasana *(Corpse Pose)*

Sava is a corpse. In this pose, we symbolically die to our former self. Your body sleeps and your mind watches.

Basic Version (also described on p. 115, under "Mountain Pose: The Four *Tadasanas*"): Lie down on your back with your legs bent and your feet flat on the floor. Place a small pillow or folded blanket underneath your head so that your neck is well supported and your chin can drop below the level of your forehead. Rest your elbows next to your sides, palms facing upward. Roll your shoulder blades down, retaining the broadness in your back. Lift your pelvis and slightly tuck your buttocks toward your heels.

Then straighten your arms and legs along the floor. (If your lower back hurts, support your knees with a bolster.) Take a moment to let your legs fall open and your arms to spread from the sides of your rib cage. Cultivate an expansive feeling, as if you were filling the whole room.

Set a timer for fifteen to twenty minutes, cover your eyes, and consciously settle down. (It takes at least fifteen minutes to relax deeply.)

Bring your attention to your legs. For several breaths, notice how they recede into the ground. Then shift your attention to your arms and watch them also recede. As the organs of action slip into stillness, focus on your body's subtler movements—the beat of your heart, the rise and fall of your belly, and the rhythm of your breath as it gently rocks the tension out of your body.

Then completely let go. Relinquish any controlled breathing, allow your body to melt into the floor, and observe your thoughts as if they were clouds drifting in the sky.

As your mind interiorizes, you will gradually notice three distinct changes. The first is physical-body lightness. While your weight drops more and more into the floor (supported by the floor), your energy-body rebounds.

In the second you become your body's witness. There it is spread-eagled on the floor as you watch the slow motion of your breath, the increased sense of receding, and the simultaneous lightening of your life force. It could as easily be someone else's body whose fluctuations in space you observe.

The third is the same as the second only here it relates to the mind. Suddenly you are witness not only to your body, but to your mind observing your body. Both now seem to belong to another person.

At this point you might reflect, "If I am not my body and I am not my mind . . ."

When the timer rings, begin to reinhabit the body. Inhale deeply, then exhale and curl your knees to your chest. Roll to the right, allowing the eye pillow to fall off by itself, and use your arms to push up to a sitting position. Keep your neck hanging, fully relaxed, until your body is entirely straight. Then, using the full palm of your hand (not just your fingertips), gently press your head upright.

Remember, conscious breath leads to conscious surrender.

Ultrasupported Version (especially restorative for the lower back): Begin by finding a piece of furniture that allows your thighs and shins to form a ninety-degree angle as your lower back is supported by the floor. Swing your legs up. Prop your head and neck with a small, firm pillow. When you are settled, place a sandbag (see "Yoga Props, Yoga Clothes," p. 56) on your abdomen and gently cover your eyes. It is important to stay warm, so consider using a blanket, sweater, socks. Set your timer for fifteen to thirty minutes and breathe and release as instructed above.

Think of your *hatha yoga* practice as preparation for the *real* yoga of *savasana,* and *savasana* as preparation for the even deeper yoga of writing.

WRITING *ASANA*

Drama *and* Karma *Both Mean "Action"*

〰️

The sages taught that while attachments are ubiquitous, there are four major types: material objects or sensory pleasures; opinions, beliefs, views, and theories; *dharma* practice (when it gets too comfortable); and "I," "me," "mine"—addiction to a sense of "self." Reader, please pause and consider what, for you, is a specific example of each.

"Letting go" is less about *you* letting go than the unwholesome mental formations (let's say) letting go of you. A concentrated mind cannot contain them. If you observe without reacting, they will fall away on their own. (Try focusing on the breath.)

Mentally play with this idea, distinguishing between the suffering derived from attachment and the suffering added to suffering by embroiling it with drama. Demonstrate your understanding either comically (by writing a spoof) or tragically (by writing a one-act piece for theater).

Note: The above dynamic (suffering piggybacked to suffering) is a bit like pride. One endeavors to accomplish something, works hard, accomplishes it (up to here one is full of concentration and wholehearted effort), and then POW. The heat is off and pride sweeps in. After a heart-wrenching scene in a murder mystery, all ends happily-ever-after. *That's* when we cry. These three (drama, pride, aftertears) are similar.

WRITING *ASANA*

A Deeper State of Empty

❦

Contemplate vast space as a lived experience (a lived *being*) or a gentle welcoming source of refuge (welcoming ourselves to ourselves). From the point of view of vast space, how is *samsara* (the phenomenal world, as opposed to the transcendental) manifested as a lack of spaciousness (darkness)?

No solutions need be proposed, only openness of thought. As in dance, writing that openness.

IMMERSION 3: ATTENDING PRACTICE

Using Nondiscriminative Hearing to Cultivate Unwavering Attention

If you can listen in this way, listen with ease,
without strain, you will find an extraordinary
change taking place within you, a change that
comes without your volition, without your asking;
and in that change there is great beauty and
depth of insight.

J. KRISHNAMURTI

O NOBLE WARRIORS

The *Rig Veda* teaches that the Word is at the summit of the sky. Polestar = *Vag Devi*, the supreme (still) point of consciousness around which all existence revolves.

Vag Devi, the supreme wordless Word, is the source of all mantras.

All mantras lead back through the four levels of sound to their source in the living silence that contains all knowledge.[7]

Beyond these four levels is transcendent, undisturbed, living intelligence (*Vag Devi*), Goddess of the Word.

In the beginning, God was alone. Except for the Word. She (the Word) united with Him (the creator), left, gave birth to all beings, then returned to the creator.[8]

Like the sun and the moon. On the new moon it appears as if God (the sun) is alone. But in reality, the Word (the moon) is with Him. As the moon moves away, it grows larger (like a pregnant woman's belly). When it's farthest away, it "gives birth." Gradually its crescent gets smaller, until the moon again unites with the sun on the next new-moon day.

Just as the moon's light is really reflected sun, God and the Word are the same.

WRITING *ASANA*

Live in OM

❧

The mind that concentrates on how increments of sound and meaning and intellect may be made into something exciting and revelatory is a trained mind.

ANNE WALDMAN

To quiet your mind, reside in your ears. Close your eyes. Permit yourself to hear what naturally arises from within. The focus must be on listening not only to your heart, but to your process in awakening it.

When an effect is experienced, there is an associated vibration. And where there is vibration, there is sound. It is said that creation (at the beginning) was a vibration of a particular kind. Then arose the auspicious humming in the form of the syllable OM.

OM = the entire universe. Its four parts—*a* + *u* + *m* + a soundless pause—correlate respectively to the waking state, the dream state, deep sleep, and silence. OM is pure consciousness.

Because OM is hummed, it is known as the *pranava* (the esoteric designation of the sacred syllable OM, which is recited with a nasalized hum). "Live in OM," says Swami Sivananda of Rishikesh, wishing his students to allow themselves to be carried by its current to the sacred Reality behind it. Patanjali too recommends the *pranava* as an excellent means for turning the mind inward and eliminating obstacles on the yogic path.

Understanding the vibratory nature of existence is fundamental to Mantra Yoga,[9] the discipline employing sound as a means of spiritual transformation. According to this school, all perceptible sounds ultimately derive from the "sonic Absolute," the eternal Word embodied (for example) in the sacred utterances of the *Vedas.* The quintessence of Vedic revelation is the monosyllable OM, which reverberates in the depths of the human heart and cosmos.

And how might a writer make OM serve his purposes? The above notwithstanding, OM is a state of mind. When you sit down to write (having assumed a comfortable, straight spine), turn your mind to OM. Hum it for some minutes. Gradually, your own (personal) version of the sacred sound will emerge. As a writer, become its scribe.

PREWRITING AND WRITING *ASANAS*

A Linked Series

⚜

What is it not to understand intellectually but to be so neutral that the listener becomes the sound?

RODNEY YEE

For a writer, to align his mind with the forces of the universe ("to be so neutral that he *becomes* the sound"), he must first align his body. In this way he ensures that his writing will emerge from the body of light.

Intense stretch (*uttanasana*) aids intense alignment.

Ut means "deliberate" or "intense." *Tana* means "stretch." This linked series explores intense stretching as it occurs in three different planes: standing, seated, and reclined.

STANDING FORWARD BEND

In this version your body weight pulls you down. The forward tilt in the pelvis stretches and releases the hamstrings, allowing the spine to drop.

From standing, exhale and bend from the hips (not the

waist), making sure that your weight is balanced evenly over both feet. Keeping your legs straight, draw your kneecaps up, and consciously extend your toes. Slowly fold your torso until your fingertips reach your knees, your shins, or, for flexible people, the floor. Initially the hands are placed in front of the feet (or, alternately, on a block support), then at both sides. Later they can be positioned farther back, past the legs, so the arms can be fully extended and the forehead rested on the shins.

Separate your ankles to free your lower back, distributing your body (front to back) evenly. Hold for ten to twenty deep, full breaths.

Note: The supported *uttanasana* (leaning the buttocks against a wall) can be a useful way to practice, as it stabilizes balance. A sandbag placed on the lower lumbar spine (for people with tight hamstrings) encourages the pelvis and lower back to move.

SEATED FORWARD BEND

Begin in Staff Pose, with legs extended straight in front of you, hands next to hips, fingers pointing footward, and spine elongating up. Manually pull the flesh of your buttocks, one side at a time, backward, releasing your sitting bones. Take a few breaths, lift, then fold slowly forward over the hip joints. As your fingers creep ahead, keep your elbows to the sides. Feel the energy rise along your legs, up through your waist to the topmost areas of your spine. Hold for ten to twenty breaths.

RECLINED FORWARD BEND

Note: This pose can be difficult for stiff people.

Begin by lying on the floor, arms at your sides, palms facing down. Exhale. Lift your buttocks off the floor, bringing your knees to your chest. Place your hands on the small of your back and raise your hips till your torso is perpendicular to the floor and your thighs are above your face. Bring your bent knees over your forehead before you lower your legs to the floor. Consciously lift your sternum to your chin.

Then hold your feet from the outside, toes on the floor, and pull the sacrum as close to the floor as possible. Focus on your breath, inhaling and exhaling evenly. Fill your back with breath for ten to twenty counts.

"I find weight in the phrases, not on them; they are not burdened; rather each has its own volume and density, can attract the phrases around them or be inert and integral," said poet David Sheidlower in a critique of a poetry chapbook.

Respond to the above commentary from a self-reflective, philosophical, visceral, or entirely imaginative perspective.

WRITING *ASANA*

Stepping into the Current of Grace Descending

When you write, there are times when sounds and shapes bring stability and calm. Meditating on this, you may realize that it is not that at other times these sounds and shapes cease to exist (or even that they do not reach your senses), but that you get distracted.

Sounds and breath can be condensed into words that ebb and flow into images. Capture one, then try to capture your state of mind as it drifts in and out of focus.

Take, for example, birds. A covey may cry. Track your mind as it repels, forgives, becomes curious, absorbs. A robin chirps. An owl hoots. How does your mind enter and depart from these experiences?

Remember, the meaning is not in the words. It responds to the arrival of energy.

WRITING *ASANA*

Jewel of Sound

This *asana* uses listening as a vessel for attending. By allowing sound to wash over you without disruption, you restore the mind to simplicity, peace, and poise.

First, do an aural inventory (simply notice what you are hearing). Some sounds arise and disappear, other reoccur. Observe their distinctive qualities and your associations to them. If you attach meaning to these associations (or to a reverie that is triggered), note this as well without dwelling on or judging it.

Use your ears like giant antennas to survey the surrounding din. At the same time, cultivate a sense of nonclinging

---

**Nadis:* channels or currents. See "One Breath at a Time," p. 148, for further explanation of *nadis* and "She Who Is Coiled," p. 198, for further explanation of *kundalini.*

awareness. As each location has its own unique "sound signature," isolate and articulate the one you find most compelling.

Watch as the array of confusion and chaos gradually slips away.

Then, follow the hearable sound into its immovable disappearance. Write a poem or story about a conversation that is opaque (mentally, physically, or imaginatively).

WRITING *ASANA*

Indra's Net

＊

Far away in the heavenly abode of the great god Indra there is a won-
derful net which has been hung by some cunning artificer in such a
manner that it stretches out indefinitely in all directions. In accordance
with the extravagant tastes of deities, the artificer has hung a single
glittering jewel at the net's every node, and since the net itself is infinite
in dimension, the jewels are infinite in number. There hang the jewels
glittering like stars of the first magnitude, a wonderful sight to behold.
If we now arbitrarily select one of these jewels for inspection and look
closely at it, we will discover that in its polished surface there are re-
flected all the other jewels in the net, infinite in number. Not only that.
Each of the jewels reflected in this one jewel is also reflecting all the
other jewels, so that the process of reflection is infinite.

AVATAMSAKA SUTRA[10]

In Indra's net is the statement: The heart of all beings is contained in the depths of one's own. Therefore listen.

Use Indra's net as a metaphor to reflect the visage of yourself, within which is reflected the visages of others, within
whose subsequent reflection are the visages of endless others.

Write a poem or story about the way two lives, separated
by time or distance, touch.

IMMERSION 4:
RESISTANCE PRACTICE

*Without the wish to drink water we will not
engage in the actions whereby we create the
circumstances for drinking.
Resistance is a mirror. It reflects back HOW we
prevent ourselves from being a channel.*

The quickest, easiest way to remove the nine
obstacles and banish their five unpleasant
companions is to focus on the only object
that never changes.

YOGA SUTRA

SPIRITUAL GENES

Regarding obstacles on the spiritual path, the ancients taught that while we all have an inherent potential for wholeness, our ability to practice the very integrative and transformational techniques that eventually lead there may be hindered by our habits and predispositions.

Using the image of a vessel, they portrayed four problematic types:

1. The upside-down vessel is a closed mind and heart. Unaware of her suffering, unwilling to accept her role in it, or unable even to envision the possibility of change—she has little tolerance for personal practice.

2. The dirty vessel is a toxic system physically, psychologically, or emotionally.

3. The leaky vessel: Due to an unstable mind, too many distractions, and/or an unhealthy lifestyle, she cannot sustain a personal practice.

4. The tilted vessel receives practices and makes progress but fails to maximize her full potential.

We don't have to build fences. Just police our own ridiculousness.

WRITING, LIKE EVERYTHING ELSE, ASPIRES TO BE RESILIENT

Asana is action in the world (skill in action). Skill means action infused with love. Think of writing.

Consider that the body is mostly water. So what's hard? If we're mostly water, why does so much of our life feel brittle?

The yogic stance = "I'm here. Bring it on. I'll let it run right through me."

Moment by moment. Not in the future.

PREWRITING *ASANA*

Camel Pose

Camel Pose opens the heart center.

- Kneel on a folded blanket on the floor, making sure that both your knees and feet are hip-width apart.
- Curl your toes under to lift your heels. Unless you are very flexible. In that case, extend your feet flat on the floor, resting on your insteps.
- Place your fingertips on your sacrum and press your sacrum forward (toward the knees, not down toward the pubic bone).
- Inhaling, lift your chest and draw the edges of your shoulder blades to your heart center.
- Exhaling, lean slightly back and place your hands on your heels, keeping your hips pressing forward. If you can rest your palms on your soles, all the better.
- Stay for five to eight breaths.
- To come out of the pose, exhale completely, press more firmly into your feet and knees, and then, inhaling, lift through your chest until your torso is all the way up.

WRITING *ASANA*

Compassionately Metabolizing Patterns into
Our Larger Nature

As human beings, we digest our experience differently. Some feature the mind. Others feature the heart. Some can take in only little bits at a time (and even then feel overwhelmed), whereas others want humongous chomps to absorb the impact.

For writers, it's important to know your optimal method of taking in the world.

By way of experiment, select a flat and factual piece of journalism and transmute it into stirring, intriguing prose.

Then do the opposite. Take a highly moving incident and report on it (as if you were writing for a newspaper).

Try to articulate how each style affected your alliance with writing.

WRITING *ASANA*

Evolutionary Self-Neglect

❦

> *If one engages in an act while forgetting about its fruit, being already*
> *fully satisfied and in need of nothing, one does not incur any karma*
> *at all.*

BHAGAVAD GITA

Perhaps the biggest surprise from taking writing as a practice is (and this comes as a gradual dawning) its interconnection with every single facet of your life. Embracing gentler ways of situating yourself in the world will, therefore, ease your writing rapport.

Let's say you're in the habit of swatting flies. One day as you are about to nab one, it occurs to you that swatting flies is a form of killing and that killing is aggressive. Since real art never arises from an aggressive state of mind, if you want to write, it would be better for both you and the fly to find another option.

Next time a fly irritates you, you stop your swooping hand and simply guide the insect elsewhere. You return to your desk, relax, and lo! A word or thought arises that wasn't previously available! Or maybe the change happens more gradually. Sooner or later, however, you WILL notice a deeper, softer, kinder interior-life awareness, which, as its source, will positively impact your writing.

Living the most ethical life possible is conducive to compassion—to making one's heart caring and sincere. For writers, living the most ethical life possible keeps psychic energies free for writing.

Dig out an old scrapbook and write a portrait of a person who exemplified this, perhaps someone you haven't thought about in a long time.

WRITING *ASANA*

The Soul Too Has a Skeleton

✒

The wise ones say:

Correct body posture means correct sitting.

Correct speech posture means correct breathing.

Correct mind means correct motivation and concentration.

Remember. Resistance is a mirror. It reflects back HOW we prevent ourselves from being a channel.

Finish the following sentence: *The thing that most often prevents me from writing . . .*

WRITING *ASANA*

*The Movement of Awareness—That's What
Writers Discipline*

❧

In the *Yoga Sutra* Patanjali tells us that there are nine obstacles
to the mental clarity that supports commitment (the bulwark
of discipline): lack of effort, fatigue or disease, doubt, care-
lessness, laziness, inability to turn attention inward, perverted
or distorted seeing, lack of perseverance, and regression.

Identify the one by which you feel most hampered and
document your past and present relationship with it.

WRITING *ASANA*

Devotion and Accomplishment—Accomplishment
Being the Faithfulness and Depth with Which
You Carry on Devotion

🌿

"What does devotion have to do with yoga? Or with writing?" you might be wondering. "Devotion is about love, not exercise or mere words."

Well, devotion *is* about love. And so is yoga AND writing. It's the quality referred to as "keeping on keeping on." Any "practice" will have periods of excitement, maintenance, lull. Deciding how you will manage them—witnessing residual feelings as you calibrate your stance—such is the bearing of a yogi-writer.

Without devotion, this won't happen, and without this happening, practice won't happen. Eventually it will peter out. (You may not even notice.)

"Pushing against" is a yogic stance. And what is being resisted? Old, bad habits.

Wherein accomplishment comes to the rescue. Accomplishment is like awareness. We heat our devotion by its light so that devotion's flame doesn't flicker and die away (get snuffed out by a passing breeze). The two are a team. Devotion needs accomplishment, and accomplishment needs devotion. Together they make endless days of joyful writing.

Contemplating the above, find and describe your personal "devotion and accomplishment" rhythm.

WRITING *ASANA*

Joyous Science of the Heart

If you could hold your heart in your hands, how would you hold it?

RODNEY YEE

The Sanskrit word for heart is *hridayam* ("that which receives, gives, and circulates"). Anatomically the heart receives (deoxygenated blood from the veins), pumps (blood into the lungs, where it gets oxygen), and circulates (the newly oxygenated blood to the arteries and on throughout the body).

One way to increase our understanding of receiving, giving, and circulating is by strengthening our heart's supportive anatomy: arms, rib cage, shoulders, neck, upper back, chest. Beginning to feel our own heart is the first step toward remembering that others also have one.

So there is the physical heart and there is the yoga heart—the heart of wisdom and compassion. Like the sun, the broader the circumference in which these qualities live inside a writer, the brighter and more radiantly will her words shine.

How to cultivate them? Ancient texts suggest giving. You can give very small, small, medium-size, and large gifts, but

the important point always is the mind from which you generate them.

Which circles us back to writing. For a writer, writing is
her most precious gift. She will want it ineluctably to be perfectly proffered. From here she gets to practice relinquishing
(the glue that seals the merit of the action)—"No giver, no
receiver, no act of even giving." Once a piece of writing is
complete, she offers it up to the world with utter abandon-
ment and generosity.

Imagine holding your heart in your hands. From the ensuing opening rest into a writing response.

IMMERSION 5: ROOTING/REBOUNDING PRACTICE

Mountain-Pose Body, Mountain-Pose Mind

In rooting, the quality and intensity of the energy
flowing from us into the earth is matched by
similar energy flowing up into us from the earth.
This is the rebounce effect.

PERFECTION SIMPLY EMERGES WHEN CONDITIONS ARE RIGHT

Our bodies are connected with the planet via gravity, which provides a reference point (a stable direction). After Rolfing,[11] for example, we feel lighter not because we've lost weight, but because we're better aligned in space. *Rooting* makes this conscious.

So first there is rooting: giving to the floor what's touching the floor. Letting it become heavy.

Then there is rebounding. The more you release down, the more the potential to bounce back up. This doesn't mean pushing. When you allow your energy to mingle with the earth's, the rebound is automatic.

Earth and body are not two different entities. Think rather of the former as a soft sponge into which the latter sinks. Sinking is the first aspect of rooting. Lying on one's back in a meadow, one easily absorbs its soothing, healing vibrations.

The release of the spine, however, is not something the practitioner *does*. It is something that is given. As tension is relinquished and joints become free, deep muscles awaken and *prana* penetrates.

Which brings a kind of rejuvenating clarity. Space in the body creates space in the mind.

Rather than focus on the pose, cultivate a set of conditions that support the body's natural intelligence.

Though indirect, this *is* focusing on the pose. The best one can do is, through self-knowledge, derive a personal list of "aids."

Take a moment now to reflect and cite the conditions that you find supportive of your writing.

PREWRITING AND WRITING *ASANAS*

Mountain Pose: The Four Tadasanas

TADASANA (MOUNTAIN POSE)

Mountain Pose is a play of connecting and disconnecting with gravity. As you breathe, your body lengthens and broadens softly. You sway, you rise, you reconnect with the moment's center of balance. Notice how this moment's center differs from centers you've located at other times.

- Standing with your feet together, feel the visceral connection of your legs with the ground.
- As your legs root downward, your spine rises, your back broadens, your chest lifts, and your collarbones expand like wings.
- Visualize a plumb line from head-center to heart-center to pelvic-center landing at the arches of your feet.
- Sense the back bend in your neck and lower back, the front bend in your upper back. (They arch slightly.)
- Imagine yourself falling, forward, backward, sideways. As you return to center, ask yourself where that is.

In *tadasana*, the *asana* (seat of the pose) is your feet. Lift them, one at a time, and as you reset them down, feel on your skin the texture of the floor.

Keeping the four corners of the feet grounded, lift your toes and fan them wide. Maintain the space between each toe as you lower them back to the floor, one by one, beginning with the baby toe.

PLANK POSE

Starting on your hands and knees, fingers pointing forward, align your shoulders directly above your hands, and your pelvis between your legs and torso. (Your body will look like a plank, raised arm-length high, parallel to the floor.)

Gaze forward. As your front body lengthens (chest opening), your back body stays broad and firm, and your tailbone reaches toward elongated heels. Become aware of both ends of your arms—the upper parts in their sockets and wrists pressing into the base of the second finger of your widely spread hands.

Plank Pose is a horizontal version of Mountain Pose. What does horizontal mean to you? Internally? Externally? Experiment with taking yourself out of the pose in various directions to more fully experience the nuances of being in it. Then compose a story from a "flattened" perspective—for example, using flattened language, flattened plot, flattened characters, and so forth.

SAVASANA (CORPSE POSE)

Lie on your back with your knees bent, feet on the ground, and arms resting at your sides. Retaining the broadness between your shoulder blades, lift your pelvis and stretch your tailbone toward your feet. Straighten your arms and legs along the floor, feet about a foot apart. (Your palms should be facing upward about eight inches from your hips.) Allow your legs and feet to completely relax and roll away from each other.

As you breathe, observe your arms and legs lower into the ground. Your body quiets. Is there any movement that remains? The beat of your heart, the rise and fall of your breath, your belly, your chest—align your consciousness with these rhythms, noticing any contradictory ones.

Let your tongue drop to the bottom of your mouth and release your jaw. Imagine the roof of your mouth extending all the way through the crown of your head. Feel the front of your face soften and your eyes rest in the middle of their sockets. Experience your breath, the light, the taste of your mouth, and all the sounds around you.

Notice the difference between heaviness and density. Heaviness pertains to weight. Density connotes thickness. (Think of fog.) Observe the various forces vying inside you as you listen to your interior life.

Explore this difference by writing about a time when your life seemed "heavy" and a time when it seemed dense with possibilities. Then shift your essay into the third person and create a short story using this dichotomy.

SIRSASANA (HEADSTAND)

Caution: While physically easy, Headstand is a fairly sophisticated pose. If there is pressure or discomfort in the head, eyes, ears, or neck, come down. For the purposes of the writing exercise, you may practice Headstand mentally and derive similar results.

In *tadasana* the body is upright. In *sirsasana* legs, pelvis, and spine balance on the head and forearms, forming a straight and continuous line with the neck.

Headstand is the king (father) of all poses. It maximizes body circulation and aligns and centers the *cakra* system (see "Lining Up the *Cakras*," p. 200), related to the endocrine glands. Since it is valuable as a means to practice internal reflection (calming the mind and drawing it inward), it is an ideal preparation for writing.

Place a folded blanket on the floor, square to the room. Kneel in front of it with feet and knees together. Align the trunk with the legs. Bend down, interlock the fingers, and place the outer elbows, forearms, and hands on the blanket. Elbows should be directly under the shoulders. Inner and outer edges of the forearms, wrists, and hands should be parallel. Bring the wrists in slightly and cup the hands.

Extend the neck and place the crown of the head down. Be sure you are on the center of the crown and keep the elbows equidistant from the head.

Straighten the legs, raise the hips, and walk in until the trunk is almost perpendicular to the floor. Consciously open the chest.

Exhale and swing the legs up until they are vertical. Keep the knees straight and facing forward. Extend the heels, soles of feet, and toes.

When you are ready, on an exhale, come down. Bend the legs and rest in Child's Pose, forehead on the floor.

Tips: To clasp the hands, go into the base of the fingers with the knuckles loosely bent. Keep the hands relaxed, the skin of the palms and fingers sensitive.

Place the elbows in line with each other. Be on the outer edges of the forearms and stretch them toward the wrists.

Make the forearms and hands symmetrical, forearms slightly diagonal.

Keep the wrists and hands rounded, to make room for the head. Once balance is steady, if you can, change the interlock now and then.

Whichever part of the body is on the ground, that is the base—the guideline for correct practice. In Headstand the crown of the head and the forearms form the base, the crown being the center over which the body balances. Be sure that the body is accurately aligned.

Turn on its head the premises of your previous essay and story. Feature their strong pulsation in two directions simultaneously. For example, in your story an issue may remain unresolved, a road might be taken and then revisioned as if another road had been chosen, or a character might choose simultaneously conflicting directions. Allow yourself room. Bend corners. (Don't be literal!)

IMMERSION 6: FLOWING PRACTICE

Dancing the Body of Light

The liberation of the upper part of the body (head, neck, arms, shoulders, trunk) produced by the acceptance of gravity in the lower part of the body (legs, feet, knees, hips) is the origin of lightness, and dancing is its expression.

THE SUN NEVER SAYS

What is the difference between a possibility and an expectation?

An expectation is specific. It has THIS in mind (one's current state is held hostage).

Whereas embracing a possibility requires an act of faith. Decisions become intuitive (which feels lovely).

The ability to respond rather than react defines being open (to possibilities) versus attached (to expectations). Especially from others. Sri Yukteswar once said to his disciple Paramahansa Yogananda, "Expect everything from yourself. Nothing from others." But few of us remember to do this.

One assumes one knows what one is seeking (that it has a certain form). But in reality, one needs to stay with what is happening, not bias oneself and contrive circumstances to fit.

For writers, self-judgments, comparisons, goals . . . it's safer to "go with the flow" (focus on one's process).

If you keep your gaze gently focused downward, your mind will drift inside rather than out and about, constantly getting distracted. ("Writer's block" is a form of distraction.)

Everything depends on the mind. Most especially good

writing. If you are in an elevator, though others are around, you can still allow them privacy. If you pass a room whose door is ajar, you don't have to look inside. If you keep your mind ever focused inward, when you get to your desk, you will not be at a loss for words.

PREWRITING AND WRITING *ASANA*

Sun Salutation

A Sun Salutation is a series of nine poses linked by movement and breath: Mountain Pose, Volcano Pose, Standing Forward Bend, Extended Standing Forward Bend, Lunge, Plank Pose, Upward-Facing Dog, Downward-Facing Dog, and Powerful Pose.

Standing in Mountain Pose, inhale as you flare your arms to your sides and loosely over your head. Allow the energy to surge out your hands. Exhale and fold into Standing Forward Bend. (For a fuller explanation, see "Prewriting and Writing *Asanas:* A Linked Series," p. 92.)

Extend your spine on an inhalation. With your strong legs and broad back, continue the movement, lifting the chin so that your gaze is directly ahead (this is Extended Standing Forward Bend).

Exhale as you bend both legs before reaching the right one back into a Lunge. As your front leg hits its maximum stride, stretch the back leg firmly. Then square the pelvis, open the chest, and lift the head. Inhale and expand your lungs.

Exhale as you step your front foot back, finding the straight line from your heels through your chest. Gaze forward, keeping your arms fully extended (this is Plank Pose). Hug your elbows to your sides. Placing your weight at the base of your second finger, bend your arms as deeply as you can while keeping the chest open.

Inhale and swivel forward over the tops of your feet. Deepen at your sacrum and lift your chest. Keep your legs strong as you firmly lift your thighs, and your arms strong to support your chest. Allow your spine to receive the energy from both legs and arms as you arch it back, neck long and head completing the curve (this is Upward-Facing Dog).

Exhale and let your legs pull you backward into Downward-Facing Dog. Stay here as you breathe for three to five breaths.

Exhale fully. At the bottom of your exhale, step your right foot forward into a Lunge. Inhale as you inhabit and expand your Lunge.

Exhale fully. At the bottom of your exhale, step your left foot forward into Extended Standing Forward Bend (a forward bend with fingertips on the ground or blocks, and spine fully extended, head raised). Inhale. Then exhale and release into Forward Standing Bend (see "Prewriting and Writing Asanas: A Linked Series," page 92).

Inhale and bend your legs up to ninety degrees as you press your heels firmly into the ground. Keeping your knees bent, raise your torso vertically, swinging your arms all the way overhead, and gaze forward (this is Powerful Pose).

Exhale fully. Then inhale and rise up into Volcano Pose (standing straight, arms above your head as if you were just getting out of bed in the morning).

Exhale and release your arms back into Mountain Pose.

As you move through each Sun Salutation, assign yourself a task.

GENTLE MIND

You might, for example, say, "In this set I will focus on gentleness." Explore what gentleness means by coordinating each movement with your breathing, and by entering and exiting the poses according to your body's capacity. Focus on your relationship with your breath as you try to keep it calm and even.

What is "gentle mind"? Observe its obscurations. You may know your mind to be very gentle but find it covered by anger, jealousy, greed. What would it be like if these were removed? Is "gentle mind" the same as kindness?

Describe a scene involving someone whose mind you consider gentle.

GRACEFUL MIND

Or you might say, "In this set I will explore gracefulness." Allow your body to float naturally through the motions, indulging its arches and undulations and the vibrancy in your muscles. Enjoy the sweep (your sense of rhythm and self-coordination). Note what that is (its qualities).

Grace can be fleeting. As a concept, as an aspect of holiness, as a kind of beauty, it easily escapes one's grasp. A cat may be graceful purring in a spot of sun. Is it graceful ripping a mouse or bird to shreds?

What is grace? What is graceful? Is it inborn? For you, what is the single most important feature that must be present for grace to be present?

Describe a difficult situation that was resolved by grace.

EARTHY MIND

Focus on the ground, your feet and your hands as they touch it, and the rebound effect of the energy from the earth being drawn up through your body.

Name six correlates to earthy. Is earthy sexy? Applying them to a character in a not-yet-written novel, what thoughts or behaviors arise? Now, describe the opposite. (Some things are rendered best by describing the negative space around them.)

FULLY ALIGNED MIND

By allowing your bones to bear the bulk of your body's weight, your muscles can be supple and free. Use them to move your body *through* your bones. Visualizing this, position your weight in the center of each limb and consciously move from *there.* (This instruction is about the "intention" of your physical action rather than the action itself.)

Sometimes we feel we are in perfect alignment and someone comes along and adjusts us. Afterward we feel off. "This can't be right!" we inwardly mutter. Yet if we look in the mirror . . . the reflection reveals a state of mind stuck with a conception that has slipped away from reality.

It's harder to look in a mental mirror. "Aligned with *what?*" (Stay with it.)

These attributes—gentleness, gracefulness, earthiness, alignment—as you explore each consciously, will permeate your body of light.

Now, describe yourself following a yogic transformation, in a setting five years from now.

While change is intrinsic to life, there are gross and subtle levels of its expression. A haircut is at one extreme. The progression of death over a pe-

riod of one day is at the other. Thus, some transformations are obvious. Some are hidden. Some are so hidden that they are beyond the perceptions of ordinary human beings.

In addition, they take place at varying speeds. A flu may come and go. A cancer may fester for months before it is even detected. Our awareness, likewise, is impacted to differing degrees.

The assignment of describing yourself after a yogic transformation in a setting five years from now requires:

1. Envisioning the transformation;
2. Envisioning your prospective life five years from now;
3. Intermingling the two in some auspicious way.

As an exercise in "taming the mind," this tripartite task is an honorable directive for your writing.

WRITING *ASANA*

Cultivating Rasa

❦

"You cannot reach lofty heights in art if you do not first discover the unsurpassable beauty in your own heart," said the Buddha.

Rasa means taste. When a sitar player practices, he begins by harmonizing with the energy of life around him, then connects to his *bhava* (true feeling) and selects one of three main *rasas*—*vira* (heroic), *shanti* (peaceful), or *sringara* (loving)—to perform according to the *muhurta* (cycle) of the day. The *raga*[12] he plays at dawn will thus be different from the one at sunset or midnight. He works with his *bhava* through notes and rhythms, as a painter would through different tints of color.

And a writer, how might she work with her *bhava* through language to cultivate a *rasa* of choice?

Note: While a wildly free-form piece would be entirely appropriate, if you are stumped, you might consider various traditional forms (sonnet, limerick, ode), noticing what "true feeling" each elicits from you.

WRITING *ASANA*

Must We All Be Clobbered?

Rather than suppress strong feelings or vent them (causing others pain), the Buddha suggested penetrating them. Sit quietly, close your eyes, and deliberately immerse yourself in your heart right now. Scrape the center and all around the sides. Get graphic. (Really dig, reaching for the gummiest muck.) Consciousness, like a lamp, thins the gooey quality.

If we truly touch a feeling (and with awareness absorb it), we can free it from conditioning our mind and our relationship with the world. (The feeling will still be there, but it won't control us as much.)

The mind tends to extremes. It latches onto pleasure or pain. But most of our feelings are neutral. When we fixate on the sensational, much of our experience passes us by.

This is a shame. Bloodshed and rhapsody might do well to share their beds with flowers, clouds, seashells. Hey! Staring out the window, carrying out trash, pulling warm sheets from a dryer also tell us something about ourselves.

Describe a strong feeling with detachment, first in a character, then in a mock journal entry written by that character.

WRITING *ASANA*

Living in the Desire Realm

❦

According to Buddhist philosophy, as human beings, while our fundamental desire is for happiness, we are beset with cravings, most of which do not bring us happiness.

Choose one to which you cling. Write a passage that demonstrates your relationship with it without naming it directly.

WRITING *ASANA*

Arms Begin in the Navel

In yoga, *samskara*, as Georg Feuerstein defines it,

> stands for the indelible imprints in the subconscious left behind by our
> daily experiences, whether conscious or unconscious, internal or exter-
> nal, desirable or undesirable. The term samskara suggests that these
> imprints are not merely passive vestiges of a person's actions and voli-
> tions but highly dynamic forces in his or her psychic life. They con-
> stantly propel consciousness into action.

While the term *samskara* is not much bandied about in
Western culture, the existence of imprints is real, and useful
for a writer.

Begin by simply noticing. Tune in to your tendencies, the
attitudes you take for granted, behaviors and objects to which
you are attached. What kind of people, situations, drama do
you attract? Other patterns? They all probably have *samskaras*
lurking in their history.

When writers facilitate *samskara's* organic process—
honoring its sound and slow, slow rhythm—positive change
happens on its own.

Consider first: What is the sound of *samskara*? Jot down what comes to mind.

Then, describe either a feeling (sorrow, grief, joy) or a state of mind (lonely, nostalgic, hopeful) obliquely—by means of a natural object (animal, plant, insect), landscape (mountain, river, hill), or condition of weather. (Do not mention the feeling or state of mind directly.)

IMMERSION 7:
ALIGNING PRACTICE

Twisting into Emptiness

Each limb, each emotion, each experience has
a center. To find it you need to relax so that
the life force can flow through a pure conduit.
Precision (honing your alignment) means finding
and refinding this organic (very intimate and
personal) place of rest.

TWISTS RESET THE SPINE

Forward and backward bending postures, as well as flexion and extension in general, always take place in relation to the earth's gravitational field, but twisting is fundamentally different because you can twist the body without altering its relationship to gravity. For example, you can twist your head to the right and left, but unless you combine this with flexion, extension, or lateral flexion, the relationship of the head to earth's gravity is unchanged.

Bends and twists not only differ in nature, they differ in derivation. Bends are impelled either from gravity or a force similar to one created when you push off from a swimming pool. Twists, however, are initiated by torque (a mechanical force that produces rotation). Though torque comes from muscular effort, its result need not be visible.

Bending and twisting differ in several other ways. First, forward and backward bending are often symmetrical, but twisting can never be: it always pulls structures on the right and left sides of the body in opposite directions. Second, forward and backward bending need not increase axial tension in the body, but twisting (unless it is utterly unresisted) always compresses structures that lie in the axis of the twist. Finally, while forward and backward bending are comparatively simple expressions of flexion and extension, there are several different kinds of twists: rotations of synovial joints, more constrained spinal rotations, and whole-body swivels that combine both.[13]

Like a dirty rag, the body gets wrung out, then springs back with vigorous (clean) energy.

The way we approach twists is the way we approach any other conundrum. For example, writing. An aggressive mind is not a skillful choice.

Sometimes when we hit a barrier we think, "Try harder!" Better is to back up. Observe, breathe, assess. It is important (especially for writers) to just sit until we reach some understanding.

For if you rush straight in, eager to get it "right," you forgo the observation time needed to ascertain how to use breath to ease into a pose (mental or physical) in a way that balances effort and surrender.

Since the main movement in twists comes from the spine (the central axis around which we balance and tone the body), it is important to notice the difference when the spine is rounded and compact as opposed to lifted and extended. Finding evenness in your body (so that it is centered with less torque) is also worth exploring. Because a twist is not externally symmetrical, you must discover its inner symmetry.

Just learning where your body parts go can be confusing. For example, in a seated twist, first arrange your legs, then look to see if the twist is a cross-the-body kind (where the opposite arm goes to the opposite knee) or if it is an open twist (where the arm goes to the same-side leg). As you start to turn, decide on your grounding point and, from there, your direction.

Move into the twist on an exhalation, then go inside your breath and allow its rhythm to orchestrate the flow.

Even though it is good to move in a leisurely way in and out of a twist, it is not that beneficial to be at your maximum overly long. Coming out, slowly unwind, taking deep, reflective breaths. Your "second side" is a counterpose. Move even more slowly, respecting any residual internal flow toward the first direction.

Tips:

- Elongate before you revolve. Picture the spaces widening between your vertebrae and maintain this spaciousness as you turn.

- Moving into a twist, lengthen slightly on an inhalation and deepen the twisting action on an exhalation. (In turning we turn first the skin, second the organ of the twist's focus, and third the spine.)

- Stabilize the lower spine as you gently move the upper.

- Each time you move into a twisting posture, be conscious that you don't overtwist in the more mobile areas (neck and lower back). Instead, extend your movement into the more resistant parts.

- As the muscles around your spine broaden, press your lower back forward toward your belly.
- Arms and shoulders tend to contort. Deliberately re-center your upper arms in their sockets so that they augment the lift of your chest and the broadness of your collarbones.
- Invite the skin on the back of the body to spread and soften, settling with ease and relief into the earth. Breathe comfortably and draw your awareness inward.
- Your legs are your roots. Activate your feet. Flare your toes and the soles of your feet. Your toe petals (toe bottoms) are antennas.

PREWRITING *ASANAS*

Twists

Friends, being lost in thoughts is one of the things that prevents us from
making true contact with life.

GAUTAMA BUDDHA[14]

"Lead from your core, observe with your mind," a twist
whispers. In situ you may ask:

> Is my twist evenly distributed?
> Is my heart open?
> Is my breath constricted?
> Is my trunk rooted?

Practice the following twists on both sides equally.

RECLINED THIGH-OVER-THIGH TWIST

Lie on your back with your legs bent, your arms at shoulder
height, and the soles of your feet on the ground. Cross your
right thigh over your left. Inhale deeply, then exhale and slide
your hips four or five inches to the right. Drop your legs to

the left (simply let them fall till your knees touch the floor—or almost touch) as you spiral your spine toward the right. (The lower body goes in one direction while the upper body goes in the other.) Let your head follow your spine as your breath releases the tension in your organs. Repeat on the other side.

BHARADVAJASANA (BHARADVAJA'S POSE)

Seated on the floor with your legs in front of you, swing both feet beside your left hip, placing your left ankle in the arch of your right foot. With your left hand on your right knee and your right hand on the ground, initiate a twist from your pelvis. Inhale as you extend your spine. Exhale as you spiral to the right. Use the emptiness from your exhale to deepen the movement backward. Repeat on the other side.

MARICHYASANA (MARICHI'S POSE)

Beginning in *dandasana* (Staff Pose—see "Seated Forward Bend" in "Prewriting and Writing *Asanas*: A Linked Series," p. 92), fold your right leg into your chest, heel in line with sitting bone, knee pointing to the ceiling. Set your right arm behind your trunk as you place your left upper arm on the outside of your right knee.

Initiate the twist from the heel of your straight leg, allowing your left hip to move forward as your right groin deepens. As you turn to the right, use the leverage of your left arm to moderate the resistance. Ground your left thigh and channel its energy all the way up your spine. Repeat on the other side.

ARDHA MATSYENDRASANA (EASY LORD OF THE FISHES POSE)

(This pose is about your outer hips, not your head or neck. Feel your hip opening, then exhale completely before proceeding into the turn.)

Bring your left leg into a simple cross-legged position with your left heel at the outside of your right hip. Cross your right ankle over your left knee, placing your right foot on the ground. Then, with your left arm, hug your right leg, drawing it in toward your chest. Release your right hip, lean back on your right hand, raise your left hand toward the ceiling, and extend your spine. Inhale. Then exhale and twist to the right with your upper body as your lower body stays rooted. Repeat on the other side.

WRITING *ASANA*

*It Isn't Just That the Hand Depends on the Body,
It Interdepends on the Entire Universe*

*When a person connects the soul to the skin and the skin to the soul,
when there is a tremendous communion between the cells of the body
and the cells of the soul, then that is holistic or integrated practice, because
the whole of the human system has been integrated into a single unit in
which body, mind, intelligence, consciousness and soul come together.*

B. K. S. IYENGAR

Yasunari Kawabata taught himself to write through "Palm-of-the-Hand Stories." These stories are so short they fit into the palm of one's hand.

A "Palm-of-the-Hand Story" can be all one sentence. Like twists, sentences are rivers. They meander along and either peter out (just stop) or merge into the sea.

Try one.

WRITING *ASANA*

Poetry Depends on the Preciousness
of Our Existence

❧

LINKED HAIKU OR TANKA

Find a partner (or another part of yourself) who also wants to write *haiku* or *tanka* (*tanka* are similar to three-lined *haiku*, only they have five lines).

One person begins by composing a *haiku* or *tanka*. The second person responds with a *haiku* or *tanka* that picks up on some aspect of the first (a word, phrase, implication, nuance). The first person responds to the second, and so on until there are at least six links. (There can be as many as one hundred.) Linking, a skill unique to itself, adds a richly evocative dimension to an otherwise solitary stanza. (When a linked series rings changes upon the preceding stanza's content and imagery, it is called *renga*.)

THE FIRST PETAL

The first petal
Has not yet fallen
From the plum blossoms—
I'd like you to watch with me
For each branch will soon be green

> *Rat-damaged trees—*
> *To reach the oozing sap*
> *Red-and-black Kamehamehas*
> *Clobber one another*
> *I watch with you in mind*

Both this clear-cut slope
And the other side of the mountain
Where the owls now live
Have heard me sob at dusk
When I was alone

> *As a girl I combed the sea*
> *Extracting from the surf*
> *Its rich advice. Today*
> *Neither the sea*
> *Nor my tears are reachable*

Though none of my words
Can smooth the sand or feed
The diving scoters
I could show you a tide pool
Where anemones undulate

I once tried to scold
A telescope moor
For harassing the shubunkin
New to my tank. Do you
Think it did any good?

—DAVID RICE

—GAIL SHER

IMMERSION 8: RESTORATIVE PRACTICE

*Breath, the primary igniter of tapas,
forms the true bridge between the physical body
and the body of light.*

Yogic texts speak of five different kinds of
breath in the body that move in different ways
and in different areas: *apana, samana, prana, udana,*
and *vyana.* Mr. Iyengar says that learning to bring
the five *vayus* into balance in the practice of *asana*
enables the practitioner to arrive at the core of
an *asana* practice in which *asanas* are no longer
performed only at the physical level, but
with judiciousness and with a peaceful
and tranquil mind.

ONE BREATH AT A TIME

In Utah the amazing rock formations are sculpted by the wind. Air is the artist. If you want to change bones (for a writer, read "entrenched bad habits"), simply breathe.

When Milton sang of humanity's fall from Paradise, instead of God he called for *Thou O Spirit.* Which makes sense. The root of *spirit* (like the root of *inspiration*) is the Latin *spirare* (to breathe) or *spiritus* (the breath of life).

Breath (*prana*) is "the *chi* of yoga." *Pranayama* is the art of harnessing the breath, which vitalizes the body, concentration, and awareness.

Pranayama is composed of *prana* ("life force") + *ayama* ("extension").

Its purview covers *prana* currents + serpent power (*kundalini-shakti*—see "She Who Is Coiled," p. 198), which circulate through the energy-body along pathways called *nadis.* The three most important are the central *sushumna-nadi* and the two *nadis* twisting, helical-fashion, around it—the *ida-nadi* on the left and the *pingala-nadi* on the right. All *nadis* originate in the "bulb" (*kanda*) located at the *muladhara-cakra* (see "Lining

Up the *Cakras*," p. 200) and from there, spread through the entire body.

The first task of breath control is to regulate these various life currents. The second is to guide the life force along the central axis, from the lowest *cakra* at the base of the spine to the crown *cakra* at the top of the head.

Deep and focused breathing alters our brain chemistry (it shifts the speed of our brain waves and stimulates the creative mind).

A writer must breathe deeply (capture the breath in the belly), steady the mind, purify the consciousness, one breath at a time.

EXERCISE

Gently press your left thumb against the left nostril, blocking the air flow. Inhale and exhale ten times through your right nostril, visualizing your breath spiraling up and down through the *pingala-nadi*. Repeat on the other side. Then lay your hands in your lap and breathe ten times through both nostrils. Can you sense the double helix around your spine?

ONE-BREATH WAVE

Every breath is a cycle of birth and death.

The total curve of inhalation and exhalation is elliptical. In one-breath wave (connecting earth and sky) the body of light is expanded beyond the skin to the surrounding space.

On the inhale, air descends to the lower abdomen, then up along the inner line of the spine, "ironing out" the spine and elongating it. It lifts and widens the region of the kidney, the upper part of the rib cage, the shoulders and shoulder blades. Finally it moves to the back of the neck, through the base of the head, and forward over the top of the skull.

On the exhale, the air falls from the forehead down (through the base of the throat) into the lower abdomen.

At the apex of inhalation, the *prana* is at the heart center. At the nadir of exhalation, it touches the lowest point of the spine.

Close your eyes and breathe deeply. Thoroughly absorb the inhale. Fully release the exhale.

On the waves of exhalation, release tension and excess energy. On the waves of inhalation, counteract dullness and sloth, thus eliciting *intent*—the seat of a writer's nerve.

YOGA REQUIRES GOING
BEYOND WHAT WE THINK
WE UNDERSTAND

Develop a relationship to the breath as it is, yogi Vanda Scaravelli admonished. Don't impose formal exercises on top of preexisting patterns of tension. As tension is released, the breath deepens and strengthens. With each exhalation the spine grows.

"I'm given the inhalation," a student says. "It wants to come; it wants that state of reception."

With exhalation you discover the potential of letting go. Breath naturally meets the poses rather than being deliberately coordinated with a movement.

Cultivating the conditions for movement to be whole cultivates the conditions for awareness to be whole. It's not mechanical; it's reflective.

Minds get excited. Or, oppositely, they sink. The antidote is clear, focused attention, first on breath, then on the object of one's writing.

PREWRITING *ASANA*

Breathing Toward Wisdom

The word *atman* derives from the root *an* ("to breathe"). Its connection with the word *prana* points out the link between opening to breath and opening to our own natural wisdom.

Have you ever tried consciously to track (not your breath but) your breathing? If you pay attention, you will find that sometimes you don't.

Carefully observing your breathing will help you build concentration. With concentration, you will be able to look deeply into the nature of your body, feelings, mind, and its contents.

Restricting the breath can be a way either to refuse or to control our experience.

We soften by breathing fully into tightness. We face difficulties by breathing slowly through them. While we cannot control what happens, we can control our response—to open up, shut down, harden, or lighten.

Steadying our breath in the midst of a crisis doesn't mean we don't feel the crisis. It means that through our breath, we tune in to the neutrality out of which strong feelings arise.

Try this: Take a deep breath as you normally would. In and out, unself-consciously. Take a second deep breath, only this time draw your attention to the dome of your diaphragm.[15] Notice it dip as you gradually fill your lungs. Notice it rise as you slowly expel air. As you mentally experience the difference, include texture, fluidity, abrasiveness, along with other qualities and images that surface. Does the mind condition breath or does the breath condition mind?

PREWRITING *ASANA*

Three Pranayama *Practices*

Your breath possesses an innate intelligence honed over millions of years of evolution. Learn to trust its messages and all will be well.

RICHARD ROSEN[16]

To understand the importance of *pranayama* we must appreciate that the life force forms a particular field around the physical body, creating a bridge between it and the mind. Just by taking a "relaxed seat," a profound change in the breath occurs. But *pranayama* is not simply about the intake of oxygen. Literally an expansion of *prana*, it is a technique for regulating the flow of life force and, in tandem, the mental processes.

Breath control = mind control. (Erratic and shallow breathing makes for erratic and shallow thinking.)

In this body of ours, the breath motion is the silent *thread; by laying hold of and learning to control it we grasp the pack of thread of the nerve currents, and from these the stout twine of our thoughts, and lastly the rope of* prana, *controlling which we reach freedom.*

SWAMI VIVEKANANDA[17]

The following three *pranayama* practices create their effects by slowing and regularizing the breath. This engages the parasympathetic nervous system, the mechanism that calms and soothes.

When stressed, we typically breathe too rapidly. This leads to a buildup of oxygen in the bloodstream. A corresponding decrease in the relative amount of carbon dioxide in turn upsets the acid-alkaline balance. Respiratory alkalosis can lead to nausea, irritability, lightheadedness, confusion, and anxiety.

Slowing the breath increases the carbon dioxide. As the blood's pH stabilizes, the parasympathetic nervous system calms us, and sends a message to the vagus nerve to secrete acetylcholine, which lowers the heart rate.

When we breathe, most of us stretch only a limited portion of the torso, generally in the front around the lower ribs and upper belly. Ideally, however, each breath should expand and contract to its full range the height, width, and depth of the torso.

Pranayama may be done sitting on a cushion or chair, or lying on your back. For the last, support your neck and head with a pillow. Have your legs straight, heels a few inches apart or knees resting over a bolster. Angle your arms about forty-five degrees. When you are comfortable, cover your eyes with an eye pillow.

Begin by watching your normal breath for a few minutes,

fixing it in the foreground of your awareness. Then mentally count the length of your inhalations and exhalations. When you feel ready, practice one of the following routines:

Calming: Deliberately lengthen your exhales. For example, if your normal exhalation lasts six counts, draw each one out, first to seven for a few cycles, then to eight, and so forth until you find a stopping point that feels right. Make the sound—a soft *ha*—like a gentle sigh, smoothly and evenly from the beginning of your exhale to the end. Pause briefly to rest in the still, between-breath space. Continue in this manner for about ten minutes.

Energizing: For about ten breath cycles explore lengthening the rest period following your exhalation. When you feel the swell of your next inhalation rising, don't take it immediately. Allow it to gather and grow for a few more seconds. Then gratefully receive your new breath.

Now turn your attention to your inhalations and lengthen them over a period of time. Try to make the sound of your inhalation—a whispering sibilant *sa*—as soft and even as possible. (Remember, the breath is through the nose. The sound is made via a narrowing in the throat with the mouth closed.) Continue in this fashion, breathing steadily for about ten minutes.

Uplifting: Begin by allowing your everyday breath to slow down and smooth out. Then count the length of your next inhalation and deliberately match your exhalation to it. Continue for a minute, equalizing the lengths of your inhalations and exhalations. Then gradually—maybe once out of every four cycles—add another count to both parts of your breath. Let your mood tell you when to stop.

Caution: Avoid at all costs any strain, distress, roughness.

PREWRITING AND
WRITING *ASANAS*
Vital Breaths

❦

Indian scriptures[18] assert that the gross body is sustained by a system of five vital-impulse currents whose operations are as follows:

Prana: Often *prana* is understood as breath. In reality *prana* is neither air nor any of air's modifications or activities. Rather, it signifies the universal life force, which is a vibrant psychophysical energy similar to the *pneuma* of the ancient Greeks. *Prana* governs the mouth, nose, and respiratory system, and has the qualities of nourishing and rebuilding.

Balance is achieved when the rising *prana* and the descending *apana* ("down breath"—one of the principal currents of *prana* of which the breath is the external manifestation) are proportionate.

As for the other principal currents, *samana* pervades all limbs and is responsible for nourishing the body by distributing food.

Udana circulates in all the limbs and joints and is responsible for digestion.

Uyana is diffused throughout the body, though some texts mention separate areas, such as eyes, ears, throat, and joints. It is thought to make speech possible.

To help you experience the movement of these vital breaths, especially in the two lower *cakras* (see "Lining Up the *Cakras*," p. 200), try the following exercise:

Lie on your back with your knees bent and your feet flat on the floor. Raise your arms until they fall alongside your head, palms facing upward. Lengthen your waist, drop your shoulder blades, and spread your chest.

Now gently place your fingertips about two inches above your pubic bone and feel your breath as it ripples through your pelvis. Exhale. Notice how your tailbone (the lowermost major segment of your spine) curls slightly.

Bring your knees toward your armpits. In this position the pubic bone reaches (through the thighs) toward the ground, which in turn hollows the groin and allows for a deeper inhalation.

See if you can feel the lift of the tailbone (the action of the exhale) during the inhale. Feel the dropping of the pubic bone and the lift of the heart even as the exhale tucks the tail-bone slightly. (In *pranayama*, we look for the inhalation within the exhalation, and vice versa.)

The gentle rocking of firmness and fluidity (breath and consciousness) awaken this area, arousing your writing consciousness.

Choose a simple activity that ordinarily takes only a few minutes (making your bed, preparing tea, taking a walk) and stop to rest during the process. What comes to your attention?

It can be physical (back pain, a crick in your knee, feeling warm or cold), mental (racing thoughts, plans for a meal, a prospective phone call), or emotional (a memory, a melody, an unexpected glimpse).

You might comment on the rest itself—how it feels, its repercussions, or awarenesses (other than the above) that it may have triggered.

Explain your sensations as though you are writing to a lover who has been away for several months.

PREWRITING AND WRITING *ASANA*

Breath Awareness

If you watch carefully, you will notice that every hour and a half or so your breath changes the nostril through which it predominantly flows. After favoring the right and the left, for a brief period it will flow through both nostrils equally.

The left nostril nourishes, supporting calm, relaxed activities. The right ignites creative fire for challenging, vigorous ones. When both nostrils are flowing evenly, one easily retains an inward gaze.

Some patterns of breathing weaken the body, like breathing exclusively through one nostril. Yogis say that problems show up first in the subtle body and are reflected in the breath, before they manifest in the physical body.

Once one masters the art of breath awareness, one needn't struggle to quiet the mind. One can skillfully use the breath— for extra energy, for improved memory, for mental clarity. Occupations (like writing) that are often difficult become much easier.

TWELVE SEQUENTIAL BREATHS

Once a day for two weeks, bring your mind to twelve sequential breaths. Simply watch, avoiding pushing the breath on the exhale or extending it on the inhale. Give yourself time (and permission) to follow its natural rhythms.

First notice the movement of the diaphragm. (For a description of the diaphragm's structure and function, see note 15, page 219.) Watch the expansion of the rib cage in all directions, attending to any restrictions or dullness.

Then take your consciousness specifically into the lungs, heart, stomach, liver, kidneys, or other internal organ and observe your thoughts and feelings as you mentally rest in each.

When you feel milder versions of emotions (such as impatience, irritation, attraction, or aversion), take a few extra breaths to register these states and relax your body.

Avoid concerning yourself with *filling the lungs. . . . Deep* action (not *full* action) is the important thing.

Notice a feeling of spaciousness as you picture each pore of your skin inhaling and exhaling. Find a specific place in your body where you have a stronger sense of the breath and watch your breathing expand from there.

Imagine the breath larger than the body, the skin breathing, and the inner and outer body breathing simultaneously. If negative thoughts arise, add three expansive whole-body breaths. Note how it feels to breathe in and out through the feet.

Cleanse the breath. Breathe in what you need. Breathe out what you don't. Let go of strictures about the "right way" to breathe.

Try it both indoors and outdoors. Practice feeling soft skin and expansive breathing when in a private space as well as a public place.

Write down what you observe—about your breath, your body, your state of mind, your ability to concentrate. Treat your breath as both a friend and an informant. Be gentle. Cultivate an attitude of equanimity.

WRITING *ASANA*

There Is a Way Between Voice and Presence

Seated comfortably with a straight spine, simply follow your natural breathing cycle for five minutes. As it slows, thoughts will arise. Allow them to pass without clinging. When the five minutes have gone by, take up your pen. Record whatever comes for a period of ten minutes, then stop.

Note: The point is to notice the place between voice and presence where information flows.

WRITING *ASANA*

Spines of the Spine

Sitting in a well-supported, comfortable, straight-backed posture, take several slow, deep breaths. Focus your attention on your spine and *its* "spines" in their skeletal primitiveness.

Zero in first on the spines of your lower sacrum. With each exhalation, feel them separate and move down. With each inhalation, feel the spines of your upper sacrum separate and move up. Stay with this practice, inhaling and exhaling, enjoying the increased spaciousness that your breath creates in your sacral spine.

Now shift your attention to your thoracic spines. On each inhalation, imagine the lower thoracic spines moving up. On each exhalation, the upper thoracic spines stay lifted. Stay here for a while, relishing the refreshment.

When you feel ready, write from the source that opens to you from this channel. Frame your writing as a prayer.

Note: Please do not feel intimidated if you cannot precisely locate the spines of the spine. Picture where you *think* they are. Happily, for this exercise, best guesses are good enough.

MOON DAYS

Twice a month, on the days of the full
and dark moons, everyone's writing
practice must be adjusted to the
earth's gravitational forces.

MOON DAYS

Dark moon. Full moon. On these days our bodies experience extreme energetic tides. They become more susceptible to injury. Once hurt, they are harder to cure.

All these forces have an unsettling effect on the body, which can easily become ungrounded. It's wise at these times to try consciously to stay centered.

Waxing moons and waning moons have different qualities of energy. In the waxing moon the feeling is gathering, absorbing, strengthening. In a waning moon, waters move away. Energetically we detoxify—release the excess in our bodies.

It's also helpful to be aware that in the yoga texts, Monday, Wednesday, Thursday, and Friday are thought to be dominated by the moon's more receptive energy. Tuesday, Saturday, and Sunday are dominated by the sun (which is more active). If you sit at your desk in a cross-legged posture, at the beginning of your practice (no matter which—sun or moon—is dominant), fold your right leg in toward your thigh first, to open up the left (more receptive) side of your body (by the pressure of the right heel on the left groin).

If the breath is calm, the mind will be quiet.

There is a difference, however, between the gross breath and the energy breath (*prana*). They actually move in opposite directions. For example, when you inhale, the gross breath moves upward while the energetic breath moves downward.

On moon days, you need to approach your practice with slightly more care. You might take a longer time settling in. You might prepare yourself beforehand for the eventuality of writing nothing. (Forcing is not a good idea.) Ideally you'd want to sit comfortably with a straight spine and wait for your words. (You'd do this anyway, but make a special point of it on a moon day.)

The day after a moon day asks for the same routine. If you pay close attention, you will know intuitively when you can let up.

If you are practicing writing asanas, *moon days are good for "long holds." Choose one toward which you feel deeply drawn and linger with it. Allow yourself to descend into your words——to enwrap each and every syllable.*

Spread yourself out, as if you were butter.

WRITING *ASANA*

The Investigation of Dharmas

꧁

During the years that Edward G. Seidensticker was translating *The Tale of Genji,* he kept a journal of his daily life and concerns regarding its rendering. The warp and weft of courtly life wound into his private one, creating a fabric of fascinating intricacy.

Establish a writer's yoga journal. Include the date, the waxing and waning moon, along with various other major personal landmarks (age, state of health, menstrual cycle, quality of sleep)—anything that may have adversely or favorably affected your writing.

Your gift (by processing your process) will be an additional layer of perspective.

SECRET TEACHING OF THE WHITEST HORSE

If again and again we examine the mind,

Which cannot be examined,

We see that which cannot be seen,

with total clarity, just as it is.

May the faultless mind,

freed from all doubts

About being and not being, recognize itself.

THE THIRD KARMAPA, RANGJUNG DORJE

DEVOTION IS KNOWING
THAT YOU DON'T EXIST

Stillness in stillness
Is not real stillness.
Stillness in activity—
That is real stillness.

LAO TSU, TAO TE CHING

A silent mind is one that neither clings to nor dwells in random thoughts. It is still (becalmed), which is different from submissive (inert). There is no judgment, just vigilance. Silence means exposing oneself to actual life.

Asana is the same.

"Every time I start, I don't even know what the earth is. I just know there's something way deep down that rests me and that holds me. I have to start anew every time, stop and start over. From the earth, I have to discover what sitting is, and then I have to discover growth.

"By consciously entrusting ourselves to the action of gravity and by letting our breathing expand, we learn to let go of the things we no longer need and renew ourselves in every moment," yogi Vanda Scaravelli says.

Poses are incidental. They unfold (or not) almost as an afterthought.

One encounters a still point and then goes further, just as going beyond words begins with going beyond the mind that thinks them.

WRITING *ASANA*

Clear Light Mind

In *The Cloud of Unknowing*, a Christian mystical writing of the Middle Ages, the anonymous author says of the higher state of consciousness found in prayer:

> *If you were to ask me how to begin to pray, I would just have to ask God, from his grace and his mercy, to teach you himself.*

But with yoga and on through the mind-science tradition in the East, there *is* a way to begin: Sit down, be quiet, watch your mind, bring it to one-pointedness, bring it back when it strays—which it most certainly will within the first ten seconds—over and over again.[19]

These techniques of mind discipline are not simply practiced to reduce blood pressure or relieve stress. Their real purpose is to develop compassion.

What is the connection? Robert Thurman remarks that when His Holiness the Dalai Lama elevates the common desire for happiness (aroused by charity—kindness to others) to a natural law, he is connecting it to the basic idea of clear light mind, which is cultivated via wisdom,[20] namely, by training and controlling the mind.

> *Our purpose is to subdue the mind. Whatever we do is*
> *to deal with our untamed mind, to make ourselves calmer,*
> *wiser, and to develop a kinder heart.*

GESHE TASHI TSERING

Yoga as a psychological cosmology (a map of one's internal process and its external effects) teaches that the mind has five natural states:

1. *Mudha.* In *mudha* the mind tends to see and cause suffering. Denying happiness and projecting misery, one feels uncreative (trapped)—a *tamasic* mess of limitation and pain.

2. *Kshipta.* The *kshipta* state is *rajasic* (characterized by scatteredness). One feels fearful, greedy, selfish, and chaotic, a counterproductive maelstrom of suffering.

3. *Vikshipta.* In the *vikshipta* state one makes a conscious effort to draw inward. Beginning to drift, one stops and reverses directions. The process of gathering outward-going thoughts is hard, but small successes are satisfying.

4. *Ekagrata.* In the *ekagrata* state attention-gathering no longer requires struggle. One is able to redirect and uplift one's life.

5. *Niruddha.* In *niruddha*, like *ekagrata* (also a *sattvic* state), there is the suspension of mental activity and the experience of supreme joy. This is the mind of deep meditation, the same from which writing arises.

Enlightenment is not something to be "gotten." One doesn't "attain" enlightenment. One eliminates the obscurations (see *"Klesha* Means 'Affliction,'" p. 194) covering the enlightenment that already is there. That's why elimination (in any form) feels correct.

Investigate sparseness, the concept, the sensation, the feelings it evokes and demonstrate how it might play itself out in your writing.

VAIRAGYA[21]

The Consciousness of Meticulous Subtlety

❧

Nothing being more important than anything else, a man of knowledge chooses any act, and acts it out as if it matters to him. His controlled folly makes him say that what he does matters and makes him act as if it did, and yet he knows that it doesn't; so when he fulfills his acts he retreats in peace, and whether his acts were good or bad, worked or didn't, is in no way part of his concern.

CARLOS CASTANEDA[22]

In the *Yoga Sutra* Patanjali states that practice and dispassion are the twin poles of yogic discipline. Practice includes all the "techniques" utilized by yogis to cultivate understanding, and dispassion (*vairagya*) is the attitude the practitioner must maintain throughout practice.

Without steadfastness in our center, our stability will be fractured.

To assess the relative presence or absence of negative tendencies in your mindstream, try this: Take a picture (or cut one from a magazine) of a complete stranger. Study it carefully and notice your feelings (attraction or aversion) as they arise. Examine your mind thoroughly. As you watch your preferences vacillate, try to cultivate a looser affiliation.

Next, dig up a picture of a person you really don't like and do the same thing. As you study the mind of aversion, look clearly at the person to see if he or she really deserves your hostility. Seek to counteract it by envisioning a larger reality— that they are just trying to find happiness and avoid suffering, the same as you.

Finally, repeat this process with a photograph of a good friend, analyzing attraction and attempting to neutralize it.

When you finish, take an extra few minutes to quietly observe your predisposition to judgments.

Dedicate one day (or a portion of one day) for repeated contemplations of dispassion. What are its personal implications? Try to recall specific examples of both success and failure in its practice and distinguish the qualities in your ensuing states of mind. Can you identify the precursors to one or the other? If so, how might you implement a new tendency toward, rather than away from, it?

Document your thoughts in a section of your journal (see "Writing Asana: *The Investigation of* Dharmas,*"p. 169) labeled "*Vairagya / Dispassion*" for future reference.*

STRAIGHTENING THE GROUND

Concentration is focusing attention on one object and holding it there. When awareness flows evenly toward the object of concentration, that is meditation. When in meditation the true nature of the object of concentration shines forth, undistorted by the mind of the perceiver, that is samadhi.

YOGA SUTRA

Often translated as ecstasy ("to stand outside the self"), *samadhi* might more accurately be rendered enstasy ("to stand inside the self"). While both definitions offer insight, there is something lovely about the interiority of the latter image.

The word *samadhi* comes from *samahita. Sama* means "perfectly or completely." *Ahitam* means "that which is placed properly in its container in every respect." Thus *samadhi* is a state of mind in which all the *vrittis* (mental modifications) have become perfectly calm and still.

One trains by focusing on a single object. Disturbances will arise. When the mind remains on the object longer than it courts distraction, it is called concentration (*dharana*). It means that the stream of concentration is stronger, heavier, and fuller than the stream carrying the distractions.

During *dharana* the mind moves like a quiet river. As concentration matures, it morphs into *dhyana* (meditation). *Dharana* must precede *dhyana* because the mind must focus on a particular object before a connection can be made. *Dharana* is the contact. *Dhyana* is the connection.

When we become so absorbed in the object that our mind is completely one with it, that is *samadhi*.

In *The Heart of Yoga*, after T. K. V. Desikachar explains these three concepts, a student relates them to her writing process. She asks a question (I paraphrase her wording): "If you are trying to write a paper, and you sit down to concentrate on your idea, you are in a state of *dharana*. When you really immerse yourself in the subtleties of its theme, then that is *dhyana*. Where does *samadhi* fit in?"

Desikachar gives an example of a person getting stuck in her writing process. She takes a break, does something entirely different, in the midst of which she "gets it." She returns to her desk and quickly finishes her paper because she has completely merged with the essence of her subject. That, he says, is *samadhi*.

Dharana and *dhyana* are the same except for intensity and level of penetration. When *samadhi* emerges, the trinity dissolves into the perfect writer's mind.

PREWRITING *ASANA*

Truly, It Is in Darkness That We Find Light

You do not go into samadhi; samadhi *emerges in you. Then wherever you go,* samadhi *goes with you.*

PANDIT RAJMANI TIGUNAIT

Create a special corner that is quiet and pleasant. One where you enjoy being. You might hang a picture of an inspiring person. On a small altar in front of it place one or all of the following: a candle to symbolize light, an object (like a flower) for beauty, a fresh food for taste, a beautiful cloth for texture, incense for scent, little cups of water for sweet sounds.

You'll need a seat that's comfortable, either a cushion or a chair.

Lay your hands in a relaxed posture in your lap with the back of the right one lying flat upon the palm and uncurled fingers of the left. Straighten your spine. Quiet your shoulders. Tuck your chin down so that your nose tip feels in line with your navel. Touch your tongue to your palate just behind your teeth, but do not strain. Keep your eyes half open with a loose gaze a few inches in front of your nose tip. Breathe in normally, counting each in breath up to ten. Then start over at one. When distracting thoughts arise, let them go. Simply pull your attention back and begin again at one.

When you master counting, you can develop mindfulness about your breathing, noticing without forcing it to be other than it is. Spend a little while settling down in this way, sitting peacefully in your pleasant spot, accumulating energy for your meditation practice.

PREWRITING *ASANA*

Lean into It!

In meditation we use the breath to keep us "in-body." But meditation is not about breath. It is about mind. Breath becomes a landmark of the present because it's always happening NOW.

To connect back to the earth, begin by sitting down on it. Close your eyes. Place your palms on your thighs just above your knees in the *mudra* "resting the mind."

As the weight of your arms invites your legs and pelvis to relax, your chest will lift and your heart will be buoyant.

Mentally travel up your spine, as if you were rising out of the ground. Lift your ribs off your pelvis. Allow your belly to loosen. Your vertebrae extend all the way to your ears, so rock your head gently to see if you can feel your skull balancing on top of your spine.

Relax your jaw. Relax your tongue. Soften the inner corners of your eyes.

Feel the strong quality of the back of your body and the contrasting softness of the front.

Now slowly open your eyes and drop your vision to the floor about five feet in front of you. Keep your gaze mild and wide.

In the practice of *shamatha* ("evenness" or "equanimity"), different objects stabilize the mind. Among them breath is foremost. We place our attention on the breath and breathe normally through the nostrils, aware that we are breathing, but without saying to ourselves, "I am breathing softly," "I am breathing forcefully." We simply stay present and attentive to our breath.

Each time the mind wanders, we return immediately to the breath. The ability to return (and thereby remember the meditation) is called recollection. Attention and recollection are two essential elements of *shamatha*. When we practice this way, thoughts gradually diminish.

Here are some concentration-developing prewriting *asanas:*

- Focus on a sound—the tick of a clock, for example. Watch the mind and when it veers, bring it back. Start with one or two minutes and increase the time gradually. Pay close attention to your state of mind.

- Another version is to listen to a group of sounds and select the most prominent. Witness it for a while, then shift to another. You could go from loud to soft, harsh to mild, metallic to neutral.

- Or practice "becoming" a certain quality, like compassion, joyfulness, radiance, clarity. While in a meditative posture, focus on the quality. Begin by analyzing it, identifying individuals who exemplify it. Then invite it to fill your heart.

- Sometimes yogis use pictures. Seated in a comfortable posture, they'll gaze at an inspiriting photograph. (This is called *trataka*.) Then they close their eyes and visualize the image in the space between their eyebrows. When the picture fades, they gaze at it again and repeat the process.

Spiraling inward is useful for a writer. Staying the course, returning, and again returning to the same old routine. So that variety comes with depth, not brilliance. Not sparks, but solid rock lays the long-term foundation.

MOST GRACIOUS CONDUIT

The birds have vanished down the sky,
Now the last cloud drains away.

We sit together, the mountain and me,
until only the mountain remains.

"ZAZEN ON CHING-T'ING MOUNTAIN," LI PO
(TRANSLATED FROM THE CHINESE BY SAM HAMILL)

When the Buddha said, "Practice *shamatha;* rest calmly," he was giving affectionate advice. *Shamatha* (equanimity meditation) is a means of being at peace with oneself. Since the degree to which our mind is occupied by disturbing emotions = the degree to which we feel pain, this practice can be a means of lessening our gross level of suffering.

Both types of *shamatha* ("with support of an object" and "without any object") offer advantages over the ordinary state of mind. The first, focusing the mind on one simple object, prevents it from being occupied by anything else. However, although the mind (at best) may be free from the expression of emotions, there is still some sense of "me," "that," "I'm focused." There is still some degree of fixation or grasping. Since, in Buddhism, grasping or fixating on duality is considered the root cause of pain, it is better to rest one's attention free from focus, free from reference point, in total openness; i.e., undisturbed by emotions, thoughts, concepts, and any fabrications. This is "objectless *shamatha*."

The good side is that there is a sense of peace, of being uninvolved in disturbing thoughts and feelings, and a temporary relief from suffering. The bad side is that in itself, *shamatha* (either kind) does not lead to liberation from *samsara*. It only becomes a cause for liberation when embraced by *vipashyana* (literally, seeing clearly). The realization of all the buddhas is described as the *unity* of *shamatha* and *vipashyana*. (A further downside is that if we turn our wisdom realization into a state of absorption, there is a risk we might end up dwelling in that peaceful state—becoming attached—without really making further progress.)

The basic nature of our mind, our innate nature, is a wakefulness in which emptiness and cognizance are indivisible. To merely rest calmly in a state of stillness is to essentially remain ignorant. We need to do more than simply be free from disturbing emotions and thought. Self-existing wakefulness, the unity of being empty *and* cognizant, is totally free from any fixation on subject and object (i.e., duality).

Equanimity meditation may also be taken to refer simply to an all-encompassing stance. For example, equanimity can mean *not* holding some close and others distant (the base for developing the mind of enlightenment), or *not* falling into extreme views regarding reality—neither nihilism nor eternalism. With regard to this His Holiness Gyalwang Drukpa tells a delightful story:

Once upon a time, when Milarepa's student Rechungpa was returning to Tibet from a study visit to India, Mila went to welcome him. Under his arm he carried a yak horn. Rechungpa was a bit full of himself due to his recent bout of study and thought, "Oh shame, my master is still quite attached to these silly things." They set off but soon encountered a hailstorm. Since hail in Tibet is often large enough to kill a man, Mila said, "Let's take shelter." He entered the horn, waving to Rechungpa, and said, "Get in. I'm at the far end. I left the bigger end for you, so you'd be comfortable!" But, of course, the horn was the size of an ordinary yak horn and Rechungpa could not get in! He looked inside to check if Mila had become any smaller, but no, he hadn't. Nor had the horn become any bigger. It was due to Milarepa's understanding that everything is relative and ultimately nonbinding (not really "truth" in an absolute sense). His Holiness said this is the meaning of "big is small and small is big." Complete equanimity.

WRITING *ASANA*
Divine Walking

Correct *samadhi* (quoth the Buddha) includes three qualities of mind: stability, purity, and activity. When these are present, the practitioner is said to be a *samahitata*—"one who has *samadhi* and is able to perform every kind of duty." If one is walking, it is *divine walking*. If one is writing, it is *divine writing*. The Buddha added, "When the mind is concentrated, it knows all *dhammas* [forms or qualities] as they truly are."

Stability, purity, activity. What do these mean to you? Holding this vision, allow *divine writing* to arise.

WRITING *ASANA*

Gladdening the Mind

❦

Citta represents a totality of psychological phenomena (feelings, perceptions, thoughts, reasoning, discrimination, imagination). To observe *citta* is to observe a variety of mind-heart states as they arise, linger, and pass away.

Thus we taste gladdening, which comes from seeing things as they are. Not only the object, but the quality and degree of concentration in the subject.

Attend to a moment of *citta*. Watch as it arises and also as it may not arise. (Notice the difference in your aware versus nonaware states of mind.) Capture your experience in a way that articulates at least one subtle aspect.

SHE (THE WORD):
TERMINOLOGY

THE LIFE SEASONS
OF PRACTICE

Ayu means life and *veda* means knowledge. *Ayurveda* means "science of life."

Ayurveda recognizes four life stages that also apply to a writer.

- spiritual childhood (birth to twenty-five)
- domestic and professional life (twenty-five to fifty)
- detaching from worldly desires (fifty to seventy-five)
- spiritual transcendence (seventy-five to one hundred)

In the first stage, a writer is just becoming alive to the "thought of herself as a writer." Before this thought—its stark reality—and after, represent entirely different ways of situating herself in the world.

In the second, the writer has successfully wrapped her life around writing. She deeply understands the implications of this responsibility that she cannot, with impunity, avoid.

In the third, the writer is fully developed as an artist. While she may publish her work, the requirements of a marketplace have little to do with her writing choices.

In the fourth, the writer becomes a student of silence, essence of the Word.

THE THREE *GUNAS*

Qualities of nature. That's what the *gunas* are. Everything that is (and happens) is a result of an interplay among the three.

Rajas (motion) is an active state—sometimes too active. Even a little frenzied.

Tamas (inertia) is indolent, lethargic. Often it is experienced as heaviness or slowness.

Sattva is lucidity—existence devoid of filters and overlays.[23] From such clarity, no *duhkha* (suffering, e.g., the state of mind in which we experience a limitation of our possibilities to act and understand) can arise.

The ancients taught that we e-volute from *tamas* to *rajas* to *sattva*, but ultimately, through yoga, we in-volute. We return to the neutral place from which all three commence.

In the *Bhagavad Gita* Krishna advises Arjuna:

Sattva *predominates when* rajas *and* tamas *are transformed.*
Rajas *predominates when* sattva *is weak and* tamas *overcome.*
Tamas *prevails when* rajas *and* sattva *are dormant.*[24]

So, for example, lethargy cannot be overcome through effort alone. We must also develop the opposite positive quality (*sattva*).

Please understand that *tamas* and *rajas* are not intrinsically negative. However, they need to be kept in check; i.e., their presence must be calibrated so that they support (as opposed to supplant) *sattva*.

The thought of fame, for example, might so agitate a writer that, from her *rajasic* state she might not be able to generate the requisite wisdom. A beautiful country setting might so narcotize a writer that she might not have the vigor to pick up her pen. Through yoga and writing (their consciousness-raising aspects) we harmonize the inner play of these forces, thus limiting their negative effects, both now and in the future.

KLESHA MEANS "AFFLICTION"

We suffer, Patanjali says, not because bad things happen to us, but because we are in thrall to forces called *kleshas*. Five afflictive emotions[25] act as psychospiritual cataracts (cognitive veils) that skew our vision.

Generally speaking, afflictive emotions are those of which the mere occurrence creates disturbance in our minds. They *afflict* us from within. Therefore their tenacity.

His Holiness the Dalai Lama says that afflictive emotions are *the* ultimate enemy. Once they establish themselves in our minds, they immediately destroy our peace and eventually our health and friendships. All negative behaviors, such as killing, bullying, and cheating, arise therefrom.

Avidya ("ignorance") is the first *klesha*. But it is not ignorance in the sense of lack of intelligence. Rather it means ignorance of our basic nature. We are born with the fundamental misunderstanding that we have an inherent existence separate from others. Since we incarnate as a result of various causes, we are not autonomous. It doesn't mean that we don't exist. It simply means that our existence is not separate and self-supported, as we imagine.

Ignorance of our basic nature prepares the ground for *kleshas* that contaminate our *karma* for endless cycles of suffering.

The *kleshas* are a part of the thermostat mechanism operating the metaphysical balance of *sattva, rajas,* and *tamas.* They wait for a specific time (situation) when the *gunas* are out of whack and boom—a hodgepodge of *kleshas* plunge in and wreak havoc.

Writers are in a unique position because the way out—an objective stance leading to awareness and understanding—is our default mode. What for others might be the "goal," for writers is the "path." The mind that sees with neutrality and equanimity is the mind to which writers continually strive to return.

SROTAS ARE
THE *GUNAS'* PASSAGEWAYS

In *Ayurveda* there is the concept of *srotas*. Also called *nadis* (channels), they're equivalent to the Chinese meridians. Literally *srota* means oozing, filtering, or permeation, like a duct through which "stuff" flows.

While *srotas* come in thirteen different varieties, what's important for a writer is that in addition to the energy from water, waste, air, and food, *srotas* carry energy from *rajas, tamas,* and *sattva,* the three *gunas.*

Anger and fear have a direct effect. Peace and calm do also. When the ducts are clogged, the body-mind feels dreary. This is why environment (physical, emotional, intellectual, spiritual) is so important.

With their subtle, digestible nature, herbs enter *srotas* more quickly than food. They go deep, fast. Therefore their ability to heal. (Books resemble herbs.)

Sometimes we have to be ready for a remedy in order for our body-mind to benefit. For example, though a certain herb might be recommended, if it's hard to digest, the *srotas* may become even more polluted. "Forgo for now" would be a wiser choice—as a writer might forgo this or that inspiration, feedback, subject, companion.

If you understand *srotas*, you'll understand why "you're too sensitive" is never correct. And why it's very important to protect every detail of your writing environment. Which means your life. If you are a writer, everything that crosses your path affects you and, in turn, affects your writing.

SHE WHO IS COILED

Kundalini, the feminine form of *kundala* ("ring" or "coil"), is named for the goddess counterpart of Shiva (pure Consciousness). Her namesake is a serpent. Before striking, she sleeps in the lowest psychoenergetic center—the "bulb" (*kanda*)[26] at the base of the spine—tightly wound into three and a half coils. The ophidian imagery continues as she rises up the spine hissing.

A fully awakened *kundalini* restructures the body and alters the mind's quality. The very cells of this transubstantiated "divine body," immune to the ravages of time, are said to be conscious and of superior capacity.

How is this power aroused?

In *hatha yoga* the focus is on *prana*. Concentration and breath generate heat.

Arousal usually presupposes initiation, during which an adept uses her own *kundalini* to trigger the process in the initiate. This is known as "descent of the power" (*shakti-pata*) and is not unlike starting a sluggish battery with the help of a fully charged one while the engine is running.

The Indian *siddha* Babaji is such a "fully charged" one. Alive for thousands of years, he appears only to help initiates. This may sound strange to Westerners who doubt the primacy of consciousness over matter, but all of Yoga is anchored in two basic insights:

1. Matter is only a low form of vibration of the same energy that exists in states of high velocity elsewhere.

2. Consciousness is not inevitably bound by matter but is inherently free.

LINING UP THE *CAKRAS*

If I think of the cakras *too much as being specific to particular physical locations, then I am doomed to energetic disharmony. But if I focus on lining up the clear flow of energy through the central axis, starting at my tailbone and moving upward through the infinite focus of the third eye, inch by inch, breath by breath . . .*

A SUFFERER FROM SCOLIOSIS

Here's how they go:

Muladhara-cakra ("root-prop wheel"): Situated at the perineum and corresponding to the sacrococcygeal nerve plexus, this center (a lotus of four petals) is associated with the earth element, sense of smell, and lower limbs.

Svadhishthana-cakra ("own-base wheel"): Located at the genitals and corresponding to the sacral plexus, this six-petaled lotus is associated with the water element, sense of taste, and hands.

Manipura-cakra ("jewel-city wheel"): Located at the navel and corresponding to the solar plexus, this lotus of ten petals is connected with the fire element, sense of sight, digestive tract, feet, and legs.

Anahata-cakra ("wheel of the unstruck sound"): Situated at the heart and corresponding to the cardiac plexus, this blue lotus of twelve petals is associated with the air element, sense of touch, and balance.

Vishuddhi-cakra ("wheel of purity"): Also called *vishuddha-cakra* ("pure wheel"), this center located at the throat corresponds to the laryngeal plexus and is depicted as a sixteen-petaled lotus. It is associated with the ether element, sense of hearing, skin, and mouth.

Ajna-cakra ("command wheel"): Located in the brain core midway between the eyebrows, this center, also known as the third eye (eye of Shiva) is represented as a two-petaled lotus. It is associated with the mind (*manas*) and the sense of individuality (*ahamkara*). Since it is through this psychoenergetic center that the adept teacher contacts the disciple, it is also known as *guru-cakra*.

Sahasrara-cakra ("thousand-spoked wheel"): This psychoenergetic center, located at the crown of the head, is pictured as having a thousand petals. It is associated with the free consciousness, transcending the brain and nervous system.

Note: As a practical exercise, review your *cakras* and notice if you tend to be energized from certain ones, while others, by comparison, feel dormant. Challenge this. For a week set yourself the task of deliberately writing from those places that are difficult to access. While you may discover very old pain, it is cleansing to air such centers out, freshen, explore, bring them up to date. They carry old baggage. Which burdens your writing.

ARE BLISS FASCISTS
STILL FASCISTS?

But what is bliss? In Sanskrit, four subtly different words—*sukha, santosha, mudita,* and *ananda*—dance around it.

Sukha (ease, enjoyment, comfort). *Sukha,* the Buddha noticed, tends to follow *duhkha* (suffering). Since *sukha* is dependent upon external circumstances, it is reversible. Sometimes unexpectedly and excruciatingly so.

Santosha (contentment). Implicit in *santosha* is renunciation—the absence of desire for anything beyond one's needs. The *Yoga Sutra* considers its practice the fastest way to still the mind.

Mudita (spiritual happiness). *Mudita* is cultivated by chanting, repeating *mantras,* gazing at images of enlightened beings.

Ananda (bliss). When *mudita* penetrates one's entire field of experience, one connects with *ananda* (ecstasy, rapture, joy).

At the deepest level *ananda* fuels words. Writing arises. Its source *is* empty.

MUDRA IS ALSO
THE SUPREME *SHAKTI*

Mudra means "seal." In *hatha yoga*, a *mudra* is a specific type of posture involving a more deliberate manipulation of the life force than is the case in other *asanas*.

A *mudra* is made complete by bringing together acupressure points at various sites (*bindus*) on the human body. Every *asana* is a partial *mudra* if these acupressure points are brought into play.

A *mudra* can increase or impede circulation of blood or lymph into various vital organs.

A *mudra* not only moves energy through the nervous system, but helps produce an electrical field abundant in negative ions.

A *mudra* extracts energy and substances from the nerves and vital bodies, producing enzymes and hormones.

A *mudra* arouses and controls the *kundalini-shakti* in the *kanda* (see "She Who Is Coiled," p. 198) at the base of the spine.

A *mudra* is a vehicle of total union (*yoga*)—not merely a gesture of union, but Union itself.

Sitting with a *mudra* as one dedicates one's practice shifts a languorous state of consciousness to a more vibrant one for writing. (An ideal *mudra* for dedication is the *anjali-mudra* performed by joining the palms in front of the chest.)

A *mudra* offers courage to confront one's personal truth.

Mudras foster wholeness. There's a rightness in the gesture.

Mudras channel energy. A writer's ultimate wish.

TAPAS STOKES
THE INNER HEARTH

Tapas isn't toughing it out. Surrender is not passivity. If we don't continually stay present, our practice can turn into a vacuous ritual, the routine of a flabby mind.

Yoga doesn't have to be serious. Or (another way of putting it) what *is* serious? Is exploring serious? Is being interested or curious? A very serious yoga teacher once opened his class by saying, "Remember, what you do here—it doesn't matter at all!"

Consider the three stages of any *asana* practice.

First is addressing the shape—figuring out what to do.

Second is breath—how you coordinate breath with movement (physical or mental) and the rhythms that you develop. Each breath has an inhalation and an exhalation, and each of these has a beginning, middle, and end. In addition, there are two rest periods. All of the breath's eight parts tell you something about your state of mind.

Third is energy—the manipulation of inner heat as a result of built-up intensity. (Think of a pressure cooker.)

Vibrant words (ardent life) arise from inner heat. Which accumulates power. Yogis stoke it.

Refraining from *samskaras*' pull[27] fires *tapas*, which is also generated by

1. Commitment (to a daily writing practice, for example)
2. Abstinence from negative thoughts, emotions, and behavior
3. Continuing to renew efforts not to indulge the lightning-fast responses that perpetuate habits

Three powerful means to combat *samskaras*' tug are:

Shani (slowing). *Samskaras* are instinctual (well-navigated) galaxies of patterning. *Shani* lengthens the interval between impulse and response, which allows for reflection and conscious choice.

Vidya (awareness). *Vidya* helps us learn. Rather than seeming unnerving, an uncomfortable place becomes intriguing. What might a pattern that we secretly dislike have to teach us about our past?

Darshana (vision). The more we visualize, record, and experience a vision of a new pattern, the more real and compelling it becomes.

Insight, however, is not enough to break free from negative *samskaras*. Though we may feel ready to change, something holds us back. ("Writer's block" has this lethargic quality.)

Like a dream of danger where you can't elicit a scream, we feel maddeningly (inexplicably) paralyzed.

As an antidote, rather than obsessing on our "block" (the label itself is an albatross), focus on actions that cleanse the body, speech, and mind (particularly as expressed in past unskillful behaviors) and on accumulating merit (through generosity, patience, equanimity, concentration, and joyful perseverance). This twofold plan (cleansing and accumulating merit) releases energy. You will feel lighter, stronger, happier, healthier. Soon these qualities will reflect in your writing.

NAMASTE

Namaste is a yoga in itself. It directs the mind to identify with all seven stages of consciousness.

Namah means "bow." *Te* means "to you." *(The divine in you bows to the divine writer in you.)*

Namaste is the *mantra.*

The *mudra* is joined palms drawn toward the breast, head bowed.

The *asana* (prayer pose) is a relaxed standing position. The feet are close together, eyes shut, posture erect, breath normal. With both hands folded in front of the chest, matter and spirit are blended. For a writer, *namaste* (ideally) is the beginning, middle, *and* ending stance.

Namaste.

GLOSSARY OF
SANSKRIT TERMS

For more extensive definitions, please consult Georg Feuerstein's *The Shambhala Encyclopedia of Yoga*.

Agni	fire
Ahamkara	ego, sense of being a particular body-mind
Ahimsa	nonviolence
Ajna-cakra	*cakra* located at mid-forehead
Anahata-cakra	*cakra* located at the heart
Ananda	bliss
Anjali-mudra	position of palms placed together at heart
Apana	down breath
Aparigraha	nongrasping
Ardha Matsyendrasana	Easy Lord of the Fishes Pose
Asana	seat
Ashtanga	eight limbs
Asteya	not stealing
Atman	self
Avidya	spiritual ignorance
Ayurveda	science of life

Bhagavad Gita	"Lord's Song," the most famous Yoga scripture
Bharadvajasana	Bharadvaja's Pose
Bhava	true feeling
Bindu	dot, seed, source point
Brahmacarya	regulation of sexual energy
Buddha	awakened one
Cakra	wheel
Citta	totality of psychological phenomena
Dandasana	Staff Pose
Darshana	vision
Dhammas	synonym for *dharma;* moral order; forms or qualities
Dharana	concentration
Dharma	moral order
Dhyana	meditation
Duhkha	suffering
Ekagrata	one-pointedness
Ganesha	elephant-headed god of wisdom
Guna	quality of nature
Guru-cakra	*cakra* located at center of crown of head
Hara	navel, belly
Hatha	force
Hridayam	heart
Ida-nadi	current of life force to left of *sushumna*
Ishvara Pranidhana	devotion to god

Jiva	individual living being
Kanda	bulb; point of origin of network of channels
Kapha	phlegm
Karma	action, service
Klesha	affliction
Kshipta	one of the mind's five natural states, characterized by scatteredness
Kundalini	serpent energy
Manas	mind
Manipura-cakra	*cakra* located at the navel
Mantra	chant
Marichyasana	Marichi's Pose
Marma	vital junction
Moksha	liberation
Mudha	one of the mind's five natural states, characterized by feeling limited or trapped
Mudita	spiritual happiness
Mudra	seal, gesture
Muhurta	forty-eight minutes
Muladhara-cakra	lowest *cakra*, located at base of spine
Nadi	channel, current
Namaste	bow, salute
Niruddha	restriction of consciousness/ self-control
Niyama	inner observances or self-restraint

Pingala-nadi	current of life force to right of *sushumna*
Pitha	seat
Pitta	gall
Prajna	wisdom
Prana	the life force in breath
Pranava	humming; OM recited as nasalized hum
Pratyahara	sense withdrawal
Raga	music made from sound instead of notes
Rajas	motion
Rasa	essence, taste
Rig Veda	"Knowledge of Praise"; the oldest of four *Vedas*
Sadhana	spiritual path
Sahasrara-cakra	*cakra* located at center of crown of head
Sama	same, equal; perfectly, completely
Samadhi	literally, "placing" or "putting together"; pure essence of all that exists
Samahita	that which is placed properly in its container in every respect
Samana	breath localized in abdominal region (connected with digestion)
Samsara	phenomenal world

Samskara	subliminal activator
Sangha	community of practitioners
Santoha	contentment
Sattva	clarity, illumination, lucidity
Satya	truthfulness
Savasana	Corpse Pose
Shaithilya	relaxation
Shakti	power; feminine form of the divine
Shakti-pata	transmission of psychospiritual energy
Shamatha	equanimity
Shani	slowing
Shanti	peace
Shauca	cleanliness, purity
Shiva Samhita	one of the principal manuals of *hatha yoga*
Siddha	enlightened master
Sirsasana	Headstand
Smriti	mindfulness, memory
Sringara	loving
Srota	passageway of the *gunas*
Sthira	conscious, steady, firm, stable
Sukha	ease, comfort, enjoyment
Surya	sun
Sushumna-nadi	central channel of life force
Svadhishthana-cakra	*cakra* located at the genitals
Svadhyaya	self-study
Tadasana	Mountain Pose

Tamas	inertia
Tapas	inner heat
Trataka	steady gaze at object till tears flow
Trikonasana	Triangle Pose
Udana	up breath
Uttanasana	intense stretch/Forward Bend Pose
Uyana	a current of prama diffused throughout the body
Vag Devi	the supreme wordless word
Vairagya	dispassion
Vayu	air, wind; synomyn for *prana*
Vedas	knowledge; the oldest portion of the Hindu canon
Vidya	awareness
Vikshipta	obstacles stemming from distraction
Vinyasa	flow
Vipashyana	insight meditation
Vira	hero
Vishuddhi-cakra	*cakra* located at the throat
Vrittis	fluctuations of consciousness
Vyana	the diffuse breath circulating in all the limbs
Yama	outer or moral observances
Yoga	union
Yoga Sutra	Patanjali's treatise on Yoga practice
Yuj	to yoke or harness

NOTES

1. *Ashta-anga-yoga* is the path of yogic maturation proposed by Patanjali. It consists of the following eight practices: moral observance (*yama*), self-restraint (*niyama*), posture (*asana*), breath control (*pranayama*), sensory inhibition (*pratyahara*), concentration (*dharana*), meditation (*dhyana*), and ecstasy (*samadhi*).

2. B. K. S. Iyengar defines *Brahmacharya* as "no loss of energy. If your mind is wandering, energy is lost. If you hold your mind still, then concentration develops inside yourself." Public talk, October 2005.

3. M. V. Bhole, "Viscero-Emotional Training and Re-Education Through Yogasanas," *Yoga-Mimamsa* 19, nos. 2 and 3 (1977–78), p. 47.

4. Remember, a "straight" back has natural curves—moving in at the lower back, out in the upper back, and in again at the neck. The shoulders should be relaxed, shoulder blades flat on the upper back to keep the heart open and breath flowing freely. The crown of the head lengthens upward. The chin is tucked just a bit to release any strain in the back of the neck and to keep the throat open.

Imagine an energetic line moving from the perineum (between the anus and the genitals) up through the center of the torso and out through the top of the head.

5. *The Hatha Yoga Pradipika* (ca. 1350 C.E.) and Patanjali's *Yoga Sutra* (ca. 100–200 C.E.).

6. The famous, constantly repeated admonition of Sri Pattabhi Jois.

7. The first (*vaikari*) is physical (whose power is transmitting ideas). The second (*madhyama*) is mental (the words you hear in your mind). The third (*pashyanti*) is visual (images seen in the mind's eye). And the fourth (*para*) is intuitive (grasping the essence or pure meaning). Without those four levels, we wouldn't know anything, because we'd perforce know everything at once. The Word allows us to understand one object, image, or concept apart from another.

8. *Gheranda Samhita* (Delhi: Sri Satguru Publications, 1981).

9. For more information on Mantra Yoga, see *The Yoga Tradition: Its History, Literature, Philosophy and Practice* by Georg Feuerstein (Prescott, AZ: Hohm Press, 2000).

10. Francis H. Cook, *Hua-Yen Buddhism: The Jewel Net of Indra* (University Park: Penn State University Press, 1977).

11. Named for its originator, Dr. Ida Rolf, a biochemist, Rolfing is a system of physical manipulation based on

the idea that "structure determines function." Rolfers hold that many of us have shortening and stiffening (contractures) of our connective tissue, especially of the fasciae (muscle sheaths) as a consequence of physical and psychological stress.

12. *Ragas* are not made from notes but from *svaras* (sounds in which the "self must shine forth"). Thus, in a sense, a *raga* is a living utterance. Instruments used for playing a *svara* must be specially tuned to produce this appealing imitation of a vocal sound.

13. For more information about twists, see *Anatomy of Hatha Yoga: A Manual for Students, Teachers, and Practitioners* by H. David Coulter (Honesdale, Penn.: Body and Breath, 2001).

14. Thich Nhat Hanh, *Old Path White Clouds* (Berkeley, Calif.: Parallax Press, 1991), p. 338.

15. Because the respiratory diaphragm is hidden inside the torso, most people have only a rudimentary notion of what it looks like. Imagine a domed sheath of muscle and tendon that spans the torso and separates the chest cavity from the abdominal cavity. Its rim is attached to the base of the rib cage and, in the rear, to the lumbar spine. It is shaped like an umbrella (or an upside-down cup) except that it is deeply indented to accommodate the vertebral column. Because it is thin, its shape bears

the impressions of its immediate surroundings—the rib cage, heart, lungs, and the abdominal organs—and it is dependent on the existence and anatomical arrangements of these structures for its function.

16. Richard Rosen, *The Yoga of Breath: A Step-by-Step Guide to Pranayama* (Boston: Shambhala, 2002).

17. Swami Vivekananda, *Complete Works of Vivekananda* (Vedanta Pr., 1947), vol. I, pp. 143–44.

18. For example, preclassical *Samkhya* literature (a spiritual approach based on insight into the nature of worldly existence and the transcendental Self).

19. Diana Eck and Robert Thurman, eds., *MindScience* (Boston: Wisdom Publications, 1991), p. 106.

20. Eck and Thurman, eds., *MindScience,* pp. 108–09.

21. *Vairagya* ("dispassion"), according to the *Yoga Sutra,* is the "awareness of mastery of him who is without thirst for seen (i.e., earthly) and revealed (i.e., heavenly) things. . . . *Vairagya* is one of the two fundamental aspects of spiritual life, the other being practical application (*abhyasa*) of the various techniques, especially meditation. Unless practice is accompanied by an attitude of dispassion, one runs the risk of inflating rather than transcending the ego. Dispassion without practice, on the other hand, is like a blunt knife: the psychosomatic energies released through dispassion are not channeled appropriately and

thus may lead to confusion and possibly delusion instead of liberation. Hence the *Bhagavad Gita* enjoins their simultaneous cultivation." George Feuerstein, *The Shambhala Encyclopedia of Yoga* (Boston: Shambhala, 1997).

22. Carlos Castaneda, *A Separate Reality* (New York: Washington Square Press, 1991).

23. Classical yoga seeks to purify the *sattva* aspect of the psyche to the point where its lucidity matches the inherent clarity of the transcendental Self (*purusha*), which is pure Consciousness.

24. *Bhagavad Gita,* 14:10.

25. *Avidya* (ignorance of our basic nature), *asmita* ("I-amness"—the awareness of oneself as a discrete being), *raga* (passion or attachment), *dvesa* (aversion), and *abhinivesa* (love of life or fear of death).

26. Feuerstein, *The Shambhala Encyclopedia of Yoga,* p. 258.

27. Remember, *samskaras* are "subliminal activators." They are not merely passive vestiges of past actions but highly dynamic forces in our psychic life.

BIBLIOGRAPHY

Bhole, M. V. "Viscero-Emotional Training and Re-Education Through Yogasanas." *Yoga-Mimamsa* 19, nos. 2 and 3 (1977–1978), p. 47.

Boccio, Frank Jude. *Mindfulness Yoga: The Awakened Union of Breath, Body, and Mind.* Boston: Wisdom Publications, 2004.

Coulter, H. David. *Anatomy of Hatha Yoga: A Manual for Students, Teachers, and Practitioners.* Honesdale, Penn.: Body and Breath, 2001.

Desikachar, T. K. V. *The Heart of Yoga: Developing a Personal Practice.* Rochester: Inner Traditions International, 1999.

Eck, Diana, and Robert Thurman, eds. *Mind Science: An East-West Dialogue.* Boston: Wisdom Publications, 1991.

Feuerstein, Georg. *The Shambhala Guide to Yoga.* Boston: Shambhala, 1996.

Hanh, Thich Nhat. *Old Path White Clouds: Walking in the Footsteps of the Buddha.* Berkeley: Parallax Press, 1991.

Hirshfield, Jane. *Nine Gates: Entering the Mind of Poetry—Essays.* New York: HarperCollins, 1997.

Holleman, Dona. *Dancing the Body of Light: The Future of Yoga.* West Hollywood, Ca.: Pandion Enterprises, 2000.

Iyengar, B. K. S. *The Tree of Yoga.* Boston: Shambhala, 1989.

Patanjali. *The Yoga-Sutra of Patanjali.* (Translated and with commentary by Chip Hartranft.) Boston: Shambhala, 2003.

Rosen, Richard. *The Yoga of Breath: A Step-by-Step Guide to Pranayama.* Boston: Shambhala, 2002.

Scaravelli, Vanda. *Awakening the Spine: The Stress-Free New Yoga That Works with the Body to Restore Health, Vitality and Energy.* San Francisco: HarperSanFrancisco, 1991.

Sinh, Pancham. *The Hatha Yoga Pradipika.* (Translated by Rai Bahadur Srisa Chandra Vasu.) Delhi: Sri Satguru Publications, 1981, 1984.

Vivekananda, Swami. *Swami Vivekananda in the West: New Discoveries.* Calcutta: Advaita Ashrama, 1992.

Yee, Rodney, with Nina Zolotow. *Yoga: The Poetry of the Body.* New York: St. Martin's Press, 2002.

ABOUT THE AUTHOR

Gail Sher is a poet, writer, teacher, and psychotherapist. She is the author of two books on writing, one book on baking, and twenty books of poetry. She lives, works, and practices Tibetan Buddhism in San Francisco's East Bay.